ONLY A FOOT WOULD BE VISIBLE TO THE ENEMY
(*page* 36)

MY INDIAN BOYHOOD
NEW EDITION

BY

LUTHER STANDING BEAR

WHO WAS THE BOY

OTA K'TE
(*Plenty Kill*)

With Illustrations by
RODNEY THOMSON

Introduction to the Bison Books Edition by
DELPHINE RED SHIRT

University of Nebraska Press
Lincoln and London

First Bison Books printing: 1988

Reprinted by arrangement with Dolores Miller Nyerges and Anita
Miller Melbo

Library of Congress Cataloging-in-Publication Data
Standing Bear, Luther, 1868?–1939.
My Indian boyhood / Luther Standing Bear; with illustrations by
Rodney Thomson; introduction to the Bison Books edition by Del-
phine Red Shirt.—New ed.
p. cm.
ISBN-13: 978-0-8032-9334-2 (pbk.: alk. paper)
ISBN-10: 0-8032-9334-8 (pbk.: alk. paper)
1. Standing Bear, Luther, 1868?–1939. 2. Teton Indians—Kings and
rulers—Biography. 3. Indians of North America—Great Plains—
Biography. 4. Teton Indians—Social life and customs. 5. Indians
of North America—Great Plains—Social life and customs. I. Title.
E99.T34S72 2006
978.004'9752440092—dc22   2006017817
[B]

INTRODUCTION

DELPHINE RED SHIRT

Originally published in 1931, *My Indian Boyhood* was initially written for "the boys and girls of America." However, it is easily read and appreciated by anyone who wishes to learn about the Oglala Lakota way of life. Reader expectations are satisfied through text replete with ethnographic detail about the prereservation life of the Oglala Lakota people. With description that only one who grew up in the Lakota society and culture can impart, Luther Standing Bear tells his story.

Standing Bear grew up on the plains of North and South Dakota during a difficult transitional period for the Oglala Lakota. They were part of a major division of the Teton Sioux Nation residing in the Western Plains region of the United States. In a series of three treaties signed in 1824, 1851, and 1868 (the year Standing Bear was born), the U.S. government fully recognized the Oglala Lakota Nation as a domestic dependent sovereign residing within what was called Indian Country. Prior to these treaties, the boundaries of the Great Sioux Reservation enclosed all of South Dakota west of the Missouri River. By 1889 the U.S. government, through an act of Congress, had established five separate reservations for the Teton Sioux Nation, including the Pine Ridge Reservation that Standing Bear, by then a young adult, would call home.

Throughout *My Indian Boyhood*, Standing Bear keeps the name given to him by his family, Ota K'te. Lakota children are named at birth by their parents or by close relatives. Standing Bear's brothers' names, Sorrel Horse and Never Defeated, signified brave deeds that their father had been known for: he once had a sorrel horse shot out from under him, and he displayed heroic characteristics in battle, causing the people to remember him as never having been defeated. As Standing Bear later recalled, "In the names of his sons, the history of [my father] is kept fresh." Standing Bear's father was a leader who killed many to protect his people. Thus, like his brothers, Ota K'te (Plenty Kill) was also given a name that held significance.

Ota K'te kept his boyhood name until it changed to Mato Najin, or "Standing Bear," later in his life, according to Lakota custom. In the old tradition, he would have earned a new name through a heroic or brave deed, but by the time he reached an age when he could prove himself worthy, the Lakota people had been confined to the Pine Ridge Reservation. He took his father's name, Standing Bear, and at Carlisle Indian Industrial School in Carlisle, Pennsylvania, he took the name Luther.

Standing Bear also had three sisters, Feather Weaver, Two Staffs, and Yellow Bird. Feather Weaver's name signified the many feather decorations her father owned. He also owned two staffs adorned with feathers, which had been given to him by the two lodges he was a member of, so he named Two Staffs after this honor. Yellow Bird's name was given to her by an aunt close to the family, and the girl would keep it always, just as her sisters would keep their names that honored their father. Unlike the boys in the family, the girls, once named at birth, kept their names throughout their lives.

Ota K'te establishes his identity as a Lakota boy of the Oglala Sioux early in his autobiography. "I was born a Lakota," he states in the beginning of the story of his childhood. Indeed, he was born into a strong, traditional family—his father was a leader, described as "brave and dignified"; his mother, like many Lakota women, he describes as "quiet and gentle." Ota K'te was welcomed into this family and cherished, as most Lakota children are in a traditional home. He notes how Lakota parents "did not believe in whipping and beating children," a comment that is poignant in light of his later experiences at Carlisle Indian Industrial School.

In *My Indian Boyhood* Standing Bear mentions nothing of what lies ahead for the Lakota *wakanja*. *Wakan* refers to what

Introduction

is sacred, so children (*wakanja*) are seen as "sacred small beings" and treated thus, a belief that is firmly rooted in cause and effect. The people believed strongly in the fair treatment of children, who, like the elders completing the circle and physically returning to youth, needed protection, and that life would treat one according to how one treated a child. As the first son of a chief, Ota K'te knew his extra special status early on and enjoyed his father's attention.

The first lessons taught to a Lakota boy were trapping and catching game, not for sport, but for survival. For a young boy, this meant being able to throw a stone swiftly and with correct aim so that he could kill small game for food. When a young Lakota boy finally learned to make his first bow and set of arrows, Standing Bear acknowledges, is when "serious training began for the boy." Ota K'te's education began when his father tied Ota K'te's pony to his horse and taught the boy to ride properly. All the things a Lakota boy learned to survive in a harsh world—horsemanship, hunting, fishing—he learned through play and games and observing the adults and natural world around him.

Standing Bear wrote *My Indian Boyhood* when he was sixty-three. The fullness of the story of his early life comes from Standing Bear's mature perspective as a Lakota elder telling childhood stories about Ota K'te in the oral tradition to a receptive audience. This rich tradition requires the speaker to not only entertain but also very often to teach practical life skills as well as Lakota epistemology. Standing Bear does this exceptionally well; even though he uses English, he accomplishes what he sets out to do as a Lakota elder giving voice to a living culture and teaching in the process.

In *My Indian Boyhood* Standing Bear focuses primarily on a childhood far from the change that was rapidly approaching the Oglala Lakota. In many ways, it represents a paradise lost. The Oglala Lakota leader Crazy Horse fought Lt. Col. George Armstrong Custer and the Seventh Cavalry at the Battle of the

INTRODUCTION

Little Bighorn in 1876 when Standing Bear was eight years old, but his childhood was spent seemingly far from the war with the encroaching *wasitu* (whites). Victory at the Little Bighorn did not mean a better life for the Lakota. Instead, drastic changes occurred as events culminated in 1890, when the same Seventh Cavalry opened fire on a band of the Teton Nation at Wounded Knee, where approximately three hundred unarmed Lakota men, women, and children died on a bitterly cold winter morning in December of 1890.

In his early life story, Standing Bear recalls Lakota ways and traditions that defy time and pressure on the Lakota people to change. Intended for a younger audience, *My Indian Boyhood* is an autobiography that gives voice to an innocence required of a text written for children in the early part of the twentieth century. Standing Bear's sole purpose was to educate children so that they would view American Indian children with "kinder" hearts. For the Lakota, everything significant came not from the mind, as Europeans believed, but from the language of the heart, and it was that that Standing Bear hoped to capture with these stories—the hearts of innocent children who read the simple prose and heard the clear voice of Ota K'te. He accomplishes this through vivid descriptions and the inherent lessons in all things in the life of a Lakota boy.

The longest chapter, "Hunting and Fishing," takes on a lyrical tone as Standing Bear recalls the natural ways of the winged creatures, or what he calls the language of the birds. This tone is particularly evident in his description of the prairie chicken dance at daybreak; Standing Bear tries to keep perfect time, as a Lakota man strives to in Lakota social and ceremonial dance. Standing Bear's appreciation of the perfect timing and rhythm exhibited in the dance of the prairie chicken comes through in the near poetic form of his description. Breaking the description into stanzas gives rise to a form of free verse so that his prose can be read in poetic form as follows:

INTRODUCTION

At daybreak
a circle forms
in the center
a leader
circles to the right
all step in time
all the same motion
perfect in time
in silence
every bird
makes a sound
deep in his throat
like the double beat
of a drum
in this too
the birds keep
exact time
no sudden motion
or conflicting noise
only a steady rhythmic tone
every bird carries a rattle
his tail
feathers rubbed together
time is kept
all tails moving, moving
rhythmically
together

He completes this section with a single comment: "Our legends tell of the time when bird and animal life communicated with man." In the characteristic way he tells his story, Standing Bear then returns to the practical, the reason why these stories are told in this way: not only to capture the imagination of children but to teach valuable lessons about ordinary, everyday life.

Standing Bear then confesses that, as a child, he loved to eat the eggs of the prairie chicken.

In the same chapter, Standing Bear talks about the owl and the Owl Lodge, a fraternal order in Lakota society with male membership only. Again, he captures the imagination of the reader. In lyrical form, this section would read:

Owl Lodge
wearing caps covered
with owl feathers
our faith is great
believing
the wearing of owl feathers
the showing of respect
for nature
we will be favored
gaining our own
increasing power of sight
indeed the members
of the Owl Lodge
had keen sight

He completes this lesson by stating that Indians always sought powers possessed by birds and animals in the natural world that were denied the Indian. He finishes the long chapter on hunting and fishing by noting how the child, Ota K'te, closely observed nature and became sensitive to his surroundings, and thus "he becomes alive and alert and living was a joy to him."

The chapters follow a logical progression, beginning with an introduction to the Oglala Lakota culture, which is politically and socially organized around *tiospayes* (extended family groups), that traveled and lived together, following their main food source, the *tatanka* (large-skin buffalo). The reader is then introduced to horsemanship, hunting, and fishing, as well as the gathering of plants and herbs for food and medicinal purposes.

Art and music, as well as games, are described in simple prose in order to teach how instruments were made and games were played; even in games, a child practiced skills he would need later as an adult. In the later chapters, Standing Bear talks about leadership qualities that young boys aspired to, qualities that required a leader to make personal sacrifices and to think little of personal gain. These qualities required a boy to aspire to be honest, reliable, just, purposeful, service-minded, unselfish, kind, and unafraid to deal equal justice to all.

Ultimately, Ota K'te's story returns in a circular way, like in all Lakota oral tradition stories. He began his tale by telling how it would have been "unpardonable for a Sioux boy to grow up without knowledge of this useful article," referring to the bow and arrow in the first chapter. He returns to this topic in the final chapter, when he is tempted to lie about his skill with the bow and arrow. In the midst of his scheming to embellish the experience of his first buffalo hunt, the voice of his father calls out to him, "*To-ki-i-la-la-hu-wo.*" The simple translation in the text—"Where are you?"—fits the context, yet one who is familiar with the Lakota language may read more into the question. The words literally translated can mean, "Where is it that you have traveled to?" when calling out to one whose presence is missed or, "Where is it that you have disappeared to?" when calling out to one who is lost. If the story were told in the oral tradition, a Lakota listener might hear this question as asking for an answer based on moral principles that required absolute truthfulness of all members of a close-knit *tiospaye*, including children. Ota K'te's father calling out to him in the final chapter reminds him that he is lost in many ways through his temptation to lie. Once Ota K'te physically sees his father, all temptation leaves him, and he emphatically states, "I resolved then to tell the truth even if it took from me a little glory." The theme in this final chapter acknowledges and returns to the beginning, like all good stories. Initially, Standing Bear tells the reader that without the knowledge of the bow and arrow, a Lakota boy "could not face life." In the end, it is the use of the bow and arrow in his first buffalo hunt that tests his upbringing thus far.

The person Ota K'te grew up to be was a well-known author, film actor, and political activist for his people. Today, Luther Standing Bear is not only well known but celebrated as a philosopher whose words are quoted by those who appreciate his work as an Indigenous writer. He left home in 1879 at the age of eleven to attend Carlisle Indian Industrial School, where he graduated with the first class to finish at Carlisle. He returned to the Pine Ridge Reservation, where he opened a general store. Within a few years, in 1902, he joined William Cody in the Wild West show. He later relocated to California, where he was recruited to act in films at the age of fifty-three. He starred in *White Oak* in 1921 and *Cyclone of the Saddle* in 1934. During the filming of his final motion picture, *Union Pacific*, in 1939, Standing Bear died on the set during a flu epidemic. He is buried in Los Angeles, California, far from his home in the Dakotas.

As an adult reflecting on his life, Standing Bear said, "If today I had a young mind to direct, to start on the journey of life, and I was faced with the duty of choosing between the natural way of my forefathers and that of the . . . present way of civilization, I would, for its welfare, unhesitatingly set that child's feet in the path of my forefathers. I would raise him to be Indian!"

TO
THE BOYS AND GIRLS
OF AMERICA

NOTE

I write this book with the hope that the hearts of the white boys and girls who read these pages will be made kinder toward the little Indian boys and girls.

CHIEF STANDING BEAR

CONTENTS

ILLUSTRATIONS

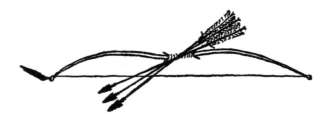

MY INDIAN BOYHOOD

CHAPTER I

THE SIOUX

My parents belonged to that great plains tribe which is now called the Sioux. But before the white man came, we called ourselves the Lakotas. The first white men to come to this country thought they had discovered India, a land they had been searching for, so they named the people they found here Indians. Through the mistake of these first white settlers, we have been called Indians ever since.

Now the big Missouri River runs through the country that my people inhabited. The part of the tribe that lived on the east side of the river called themselves Dakotas, and those who lived on the west side of this stream called themselves Lakotas. And I was born a Lakota.

Later, when many white people arrived in this country, they saw that my tribe was a very powerful and independent one. We kept our land to ourselves by making all other tribes stay away from us. Our warriors were brave and noted for their skill in fighting. Therefore, they were feared by all other tribes. The white people, seeing that we were feared by the tribes that surrounded us, began to fear us too, so they called us Sioux. The word 'Sioux' is a French word and means 'cutthroat.' So that is how we became known as the Sioux. Some writers have called us the 'Fighting Sioux'; others have called us the 'Mighty Sioux.' Our people were full of pride, but our women were quiet and gentle and our men were brave and dignified. We earned our right to pride, for it was a cardinal principle for the Sioux to be brave, and to be a coward was unforgivable.

Some of the great Sioux were Two Strikes, Swift Bear, Quick Bear, Good Boys, Black Crow, and Iron Shell. All of these men were brave and had qualities that made them admired. They have now passed on, for they were men of my boyhood. Iron Shell was the father of my brother-in-law, Hollow Horn Bear, who was also noted for his bravery. Hollow Horn Bear dared to talk when others thought it best or more comfortable to remain quiet. Then there was Little Wound, who was a great brave, and One Horse, who was a great chief and my grandfather. Both of these men were respected for their kindness and wisdom in dealing with the tribe. Standing Bear the First, my father, was known as being extremely just. In his decisions he used good judgment and never wronged any one. His whole thought was to do the best for his tribe, and no sacrifice was too great for him to make. He would give to the needy until he was almost in need himself. He will always be a great man among the Sioux.

Perhaps the man who stands the highest of all in the tribe as a great and fearless warrior was Crazy Horse. The faith of Crazy Horse in the power of the Great Mystery to guide and protect him was a marvel to all the people of the tribe, given to faith as they were. He seemed to lead a charmed life in battle. He exposed himself openly to both Indian foes and to the troops of the white man, yet he was never even wounded.

My father, I claim, was the greatest chief who ever lived the lives of both the Indian and the white man. For in his later years he lived according to Christian principles and tried to be a good citizen of this country. He encouraged me to go to school and to learn as much as I could of the life that was so different from the one we had known. My father was truly a man of great vision. He foresaw the great change that the Indian had to make, and it must have hurt him to see me plunged into a life that was just the opposite to what had been planned for me and that was foreign to all our traditions. But he sacrificed his feelings for the good of the tribe. Father was the first man to see the need of day schools on the reservations. Then he made it more convenient for the Indians to get their rations. For a time it was necessary for the Sioux to travel fifty and sixty miles to get their rations, but my father succeeded in getting the stations placed closer together. A personal habit that

I always admired in him was neatness and cleanliness.

Now, in the naming of these great men you will notice that I have not mentioned the names you usually see mentioned in books written by white men. The white men who have written histories of the Indian could not, of course, know of inner tribal matters nor of the attitudes of the people in general.

The home of my tribe, the Western Sioux, was all that territory which is now called North and South Dakota, and all this land once belonged to my people. It was a beautiful country. In the springtime and early summer the plains, as far as the eye could see, were covered with velvety green grass. Even the rolling hills were green, and here and there was a pretty stream. Over the hills roamed the buffalo and in the woods that bordered the streams were luscious fruits that were ours for the picking. In the winter everything was covered with snow, but we always had plenty of food to last through the winter until spring came again. Life was full of happiness and contentment for my people. The Sioux have

5

lived a long time in this region. No one knows how long. But there are many legends about my tribe and also about the Bad Lands and the Black Hills, showing that we have lived there many, many years. These legends are historical and interesting and will be told in another book.

A tipi was my first home. In it I was born, and my earliest recollection is playing around the fire and being watched over by my Indian mother. As a baby I swung in an Indian cradle from poles in the tipi. I was the first son of a chief and I was expected to grow up brave and fearless like my father. I was named Plenty Kill. My parents called me Ota K'te, for that was the way to say 'Plenty Kill' in Sioux.

As I grew up, my father began to teach me all the things that a little Indian boy should know. When I was old enough to be put on a pony, he taught me to ride. He tied my pony to his with a rope and I rode this way until I had learned to handle the pony myself. When I had learned to ride, I went on short hunts with him and he taught me how to butcher small game. Finally, the eventful day came when I went on a buffalo hunt. That was an important day in my life when I went home to the tipi and told my mother I had killed a buffalo. She was proud of me and that made me happy.

I learned about the habits of wild animals and how to trap them. I learned to shoot birds with a bow and arrow and to roast them on the fire. I soon came to know much about the weather and how to prepare for the coming of winter by tanning skins for warm clothing. By knowing all these things, we had no fear of Nature, but on the contrary loved Nature. She seemed bountiful to us with all the things she had provided for our comfort.

At this time we lived close to Nature and knew nothing but Nature. We observed everything of the outdoors, and in this way learned many things that were good and helpful for us to know. The Indian knows that Nature is wise, and that by keeping our eyes open, we learn her wise ways.

For instance, we were taught to go to bed when the rest of the world went to rest. When darkness came and all the birds and animals went to sleep, we were sleeping too. That helped us to become strong and healthy, so that we grew up to be strong, stout-hearted men.

We were taught to rise early in the morning before sunrise. Our parents knew it was good for us to rise early, so they began to train us when we were quite young. You see, animals are all awake and stirring about before sunrise, so you can understand that it would be a poor hunter who would start for a hunt after the game was gone. Then in early days, when our tribe had enemies, it was necessary for us to rise early if we were to go on a war party and not let the enemy get the advantage of us. The white people have a saying, 'The early bird catches the worm,' which means much the same that I am telling you. Of course, we tried to obey our parents when they called to us in the morning and we were supposed to get up at the first call. Not all Sioux boys, however, were obedient. Some were lazy and would not heed their father's or mother's voice. When it became necessary for a parent to punish a disobedient child, it was not done in a harsh manner. The worst thing a Sioux parent did was to pour cold water on a child's face.

8

This would awaken sleepy boys and girls, and they would be ashamed of themselves. We were never whipped nor severely punished, for Sioux parents did not believe in whipping and beating children.

Through this method of upbringing, a bond or a tie was formed between Sioux parents and children, so that as we grew in years our respect for our parents grew also. Finally, as we grew to manhood, we looked forward to the day when we should repay our kind parents by taking care of them in their old age. We looked upon this as a pleasure and not a duty.

Now, what did we do after we were up in the morning and our day had begun? In those days we did not have nice bathtubs and bathrooms nor even a washbasin. But our tipis were always close to a pure running stream, so the first thing we did was to run to the stream, take a mouthful of water, rinse our mouths well, wash our faces, then take a big drink. This last we did, for we knew it was good for our health, and is something every one should do on getting up in the morning. The use of pure running water and never breathing anything but pure air kept us strong and clean in body. It is a well-known fact that the Sioux people were a healthy people and were seldom sick. Most of us died from old age or from wounds received in battle. Sometimes, too, a man was injured during a hunt. When we were through at the brook and with our bathing, we felt fine and had a good appetite for breakfast. Once in a while one of the boys would jump into the stream and enjoy a bath. Then more than likely the rest of us would follow, and we would all have a fine bath before going back to the tipi to begin the day by eating breakfast. This morning meal, as did all other meals, consisted of meat cooked in one of the various ways in which Indian women prepared meat for food. We did not drink strong coffee, and would not have cared for it, anyway. Neither did we have bread in those days. Sometimes our meat was boiled, and if so we had soup which we enjoyed. Then sometimes our meat was roasted over the open fire. This means of cooking gave our meat a very fine flavor, and if a few ashes got on the meat, we did not mind, but rather liked it, for the Indian knows that a little ash eaten with his meat is a good tonic for the stomach. It acts as a cleanser and helps the digestion. Though we did not have bread in those days, we did not miss it, for we had other things to take its place. There were many plants that were good served with our meat either raw or cooked. These plants and herbs, aside from being good for food, were good to use as medicine in case of sickness and then again in the treatment of wounds. About these I will tell you later. When summertime came, we boys had the fun of gathering and eating the wild fruits. There were blackberries which we liked very much and the red currants which were so pretty when ripe; the wild plum which had such a fine flavor and the cherry black and luscious when ripe. Then from the wild-rose bush we gathered a fruit of which we were very fond. In the autumn, after the petals of the rose had blown away, there formed, just where the bloom had been, a little fruit that looked something like a tiny crabapple. They were a pretty red, sometimes streaked with yellow, and we thought they were delicious. Our mothers sometimes gathered these and pounded them and made them into balls, as popcorn balls are now made. Oh, what fun to gather and eat these delicious fruits! What fun to play along the bank of the stream and look for currants and blackberries! There were no signs here and there, 'Keep out!' or, 'Boys stay out!' All was free to us and all we had to do was to 'go get it.' I also remember a small fruit or berry which grew in sandy soil on low bushes. When ripe, they were black like cherries, so the white people called them 'sand cherries.' Our name for them was *e-un-ye-ya-pi*. There is something peculiar about these cherries. When we gathered them, we always stood against the wind and never with the wind blowing from us across the plant. If we did, the fruit lost some of its flavor, but if gathered in the right way, they were sweeter than if gathered in the wrong way. This, I believe, is one of many secrets which the Indian possesses, for I have never met a white person who knew this. But Nature has given more of her secret knowledge to us than to the white man. Maybe this is so because we lived so close to her and appreciated her so much. Then another reason is because the Indian's senses of sight, hearing, and smell are keener than the senses of the white man. Life for the Indian is one of harmony with Nature and the things which surround him. The Indian tried to fit in with Nature and to understand, not to conquer and to rule. We were rewarded by learning much that the white man will never know. Life was a glorious thing, for great contentment comes with the feeling of friendship and kinship with the living things about you. The white man seems to look upon all animal life as enemies, while we looked upon them as friends and bene-factors. They were one with the Great Mystery and so were we. We could feel the peace and power of the Great Mystery in the soft grass under our feet and in the blue sky above us. All this made deep feeling within us, and the old wise men thought much about it, and this is how we got our religion.

The trapping and catching of game was also one of the first lessons learned by the Indian boy. Before we were old enough to use a bow and arrow, we learned to kill small animals such as rabbits, squirrels, and quail, or other birds by throwing stones. We killed these small animals for food and not for sport. We were told by our parents not to kill animals or birds, then leave them lying on the ground.

For practice and also because we enjoyed it, we would select a small bush or shrub, imagine there was game in it, then throw and throw until we became expert and could hit almost anything we wished to. Even to this day I am good at throwing stones and can hit my mark. I remember when my brother got a new shotgun and how anxious he was to show me how well he could use it. He asked me to go with him to look for ducks. When we got to the creek there was our duck. My brother, eager to get the duck, crept closer and closer. I saw that the duck was getting ready to fly, and though I was standing far back of my brother, I picked up a stone and throwing it over his head got the duck. He plainly showed his disappointment in not getting a chance to show me how his gun worked, yet we were lucky to get our duck. I was the one, to be sure, who laughed first, and though my brother could not help being a little disappointed, he laughed with me.

While still too small to use bows and arrows or guns, we not only threw stones by hand. We had throwing games in which we became expert marksmen. We would select a pliant willow stick, flatten it a little at one end, leaving the other end round for a handle. Having a number of stones of suitable size close at hand, we would place one on the flat end of the stick and bending it back with the right hand, throw it with considerable force. With practice we would hit anything at which we aimed, and, used as a weapon, this stick would kill rabbits, squirrels, or prairie chickens, all of which were excellent food when cooked. We even learned to flip gravel with the forefinger of each hand in such a way that they would strike with a sting like shot. We boys would line up and play at battle, shooting these pebbles back and forth at one another, never missing our mark.

When it came time to take up the bow and arrow, a very real and serious training began for the boy. The making of both the bow and arrow required skill and knowledge. There is a long history connected with the first use of the bow and the influence it has had on man. Some writers who realize the importance of the bow have written entire books on it. The man who made the first bow was a real inventor and gave to the world a weapon that was to live for centuries of time and prove of use to millions of people. In the use of the bow, we had to become very skillful, for in my days of boyhood it was the means of getting all our food, mainly the buffalo. It not only took a skillful man, but a brave one, to face a herd of buffalo with nothing but a trusty bow and a quiver full of arrows. Also we had to remember that our enemies were skillful men with the bow and arrow. I think you can see what this weapon meant to us and the great dependence we put in it. It was the one weapon that preserved us from starvation or defeat, so it would have been unpardonable for a Sioux boy to grow up without knowledge of this useful article. Without it he could not face life.

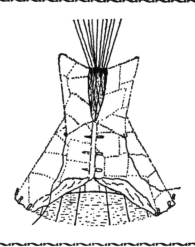

CHAPTER II

BOWS AND ARROWS

WHEN we were little fellows and had not yet become hunters, we made tiny bows which we played with in the tipis. They were just like the large bows, perfect in workmanship, and though small were just the thing with which to practice both the art of making and shooting. We used almost any kind of wood for these play bows and arrows, but when we began making them for real use, we had to learn how to select wood. That was part of the craft. Around the main trunk of the cherry tree there grew the second-growth branches and these were straight and slender. We cut them off and peeled the bark with our finger-nails, leaving the wood white and beautiful to look at. We used our teeth and finger-nails a good deal in those days. We never thought of manicuring our nails or beautifying them, but just the same they were strong and useful and our teeth were strong and white. Both our nails and teeth served us for many purposes which the white man never even knows about. But I have noticed that the dentist nowadays is a very busy man.

Our arrows needed very little shaping, but when they did we used a knife, for by that time the Sioux had knives which they had obtained from the white people. Not all of us boys were lucky enough to possess a knife, but if a boy in the camp owned one, he was kind and generous with it and would let us all use it. We measured the length of our arrows by the distance from our elbow joint to the tip of our middle finger and back to the wrist. This would give us the length of arrow that was proper for our size. When ready for feathering, we would search in the woods for suitable feathers, such as hawk, crow, prairie chicken, or duck. Turkey feathers are the best of all with which to finish arrows, but they were scarce in our country, and usually only the warriors and hunters used them. We cut our feathers different lengths, then fastened them to the arrow with sinew. Sometimes we split our feathers and sometimes we did not. There were various ways of putting on the feathers, and if we made a very pretty arrow that was more for show than use, we finished it with fine eagle down colored in brilliant hues. More than a little skill can be put into a well-made arrow.

After feathering came the pointing. Some of the arrows we whittled to a sharp point at the end. Others we cut off straight, leaving a blunt end, for it was not necessary to have a sharp point for the small game which we hunted. Then again we whittled the end to a bulb or ball, which made a rather odd-looking arrow, but was fine for small game. If we chanced to pick up a flint point, we thought ourselves lucky, for the Sioux never made flint arrow points. The flint was fastened to the end of the arrow by first splitting the end of the arrow, setting in the hilt of the flint point and wrapping it with sinew. Oftentimes we found pieces of bone that were shaped like an arrow point and these we put on just as we did the flint point.

In making bows, we often found a piece of wood that was shaped so that it was ready for stringing. In looking for wood, we first looked for ash, as it had more spring and is not affected by the weather. If we did not find ash, we would use hickory, willow, or maybe the cherry or plum tree wood, but we always preferred the ash. When we had our stick, we hewed the side that would be the inside of the bow, leaving the bark on the outer side or back of the bow. No Sioux bow was more than four and one half or five feet long. Hunting bows were made short for convenience. A long bow was in the way of the hunter, whether on horseback or hunting in the long grass or in the woods. No matter what sort of wood we selected for our bow, we took a stick that was not too strong and did not require much strength to pull. The bow with lots of spring was easier to shoot and could be shot much more rapidly than a stiff bow. Quick use of the bow was what we tried to acquire. We did not think of posing as is done today in modern archery. We learned to shoot our bow with the quickest action possible. It is perhaps hard for the boy of today, even the Indian boy, to realize what the bow meant in olden days to the Indian. It was with him at all hours, even at night. At the slightest noise his hand was on the bow and arrow that lay by his side.

In olden days before the Indian had the horse, he hunted the buffalo with a very short bow. The long bow that the modern archer uses would have been in the way of a hunter creeping upon a herd of buffalo through the high grass. Sometimes the Indian hunter put on the skin of a wolf — head, tail, and all — to cover his body. Wearing these hides, if working against the wind, helped him to come quite close to a herd. These short bows were carried either in the hand or stuck into the belt in front. The quiver, which was slung over the left shoulder, was made of buffalo hide as a rule. Buffalo hide is smooth in the summer-time, much like the hide of the horse, but in the winter-time it is thick and woolly. Sometimes, if the hunter was quite lucky, he owned a quiver of otter hide. When not hunting, the brave often carried a double quiver, one section to hold the bow and the other section to hold the arrows. If a young man owned a fine quiver of otter hide and some beautifully decorated arrows, he was quite the envy of the rest of the young men. With one of these he would be 'all dressed up,' and if he had a sweetheart, he would be proud to put it on and let her admire him.

The making of our bow string was very interesting work. In fact, the whole craft connected with bow-and-arrow-making became very fascinating to us. The more we made and the more we hunted, the more fascinated we became. Even today I like once in a while to make a nice bow and to feather some pretty arrows.

Mother always had a supply of sinew on hand, so when we wanted some, we always went to her. You see sinew in the Indian tipi was a necessary household article like thread in the modern home. Mother used the sinew in the making of all sorts of wearing apparel and in making leggins or moccasins. In fact, our home was sewed together with sinew, for the skins in the tipi were put together with such skill that no rain nor melting snow came through. Our mothers were very clever in their way and good home-makers. All the short pieces of sinew Mother gave to us, and we made long strings of them by wetting the ends in our mouths and rubbing them together on our bare knees. We learned to make an extra string and to roll it up and carry it at the end of the bow. No good hunter would be caught without a string in case one got broken. There is a great deal of difference in the quality of animal sinew. Deer sinew is very fine and soft and is used in making the arrows of warriors or hunters. But for sewing up the tipi and in making bow strings, the buffalo sinew was stronger and better. The sinew lies in two long cords along the backbone of the animal. This we scraped clean of all flesh and pasted it to a tipi pole. When dry, it came off itself, then was put away in a rawhide bag for future use. There it would keep for almost any length of time.

When we had learned to make good bows and arrows, we had learned many other things also, and the play hours of our boyhood were really a preparation for the tasks and duties of manhood.

CHAPTER III

THE INDIAN BOY AND HIS PONY

SOME of the pleasantest memories of my boyhood are of the days that my playmates and I spent with our ponies. As I mentioned before, every Sioux boy owned a pony and became an expert rider. A great friendship sprang up between the boy and his pony. It is well known that the horse is a very sensible animal, but he is also very sensitive to his surroundings, and after many years of companionship with men, he comes to know the wishes of his owner almost without spoken word. So it was that I and my pony came to understand each other very well, indeed. I was kind to him, for I was fond of him and he was kind and gentle with me. The first little pony I owned was black and to me just as good and smart as any 'Black Beauty' ever written about.

If a pony becomes well tamed, his master can catch him even in the dark, for he can learn to recognize footsteps and will stop to be caught. In many cases boy and colt grew up together and became life companions, so it was natural that each should know the other well.

When first beginning to ride, we were still too small to mount our ponies ourselves. If more than one boy was riding, we would help one another. The largest of two boys would clasp his hands together to form a stirrup and up would go the small boy. Then the mounted boy would put out his foot for the boy on the ground to use as a stirrup and up he would go. If alone, and there was no tree stump nor bank to which the pony could be led, we learned to use our wits and strength, for you must remember that when we first began to ride ponies, we were very little fellows. We would catch hold of the pony's mane, wrap our right leg around the pony's fore

26

leg, and climb as we would climb a tree. When we were high enough to put our left heel over the back of the pony, we pulled ourselves up into place. We always mounted Indian style, which is the left leg over the right side of the horse. The white man mounts the opposite way. There was another way in which to mount, providing we had a rope with us. Tying one end of the rope to the mane of the pony, we would make a loop at the other end for a stirrup. The rest was easy. If our legs grew tired from riding long distances, we would take a rope and loop it at two ends and throw it over the back of the pony in front of us and put our feet in the loops.

Sometimes it was necessary for us to break a wild pony to ride. There was danger that we would get kicked or in some way receive an injury, but we were strong and quick on our feet. There were many ways in which to break a pony and get him used to our presence. One way was to drive the wild ponies into deep water, swim up to them, and, catching hold of either tail or mane, play with them. We were all good swimmers, and anyway, horses in the water cannot kick hard, so there was little danger of our getting hurt. We would not be rough with the animals, but just play with them until they were used to us and could see that we would not harm them. After a while we ventured to climb on their backs and they didn't seem to mind at all.

White men in breaking horses are often rough and cruel, but in all the methods we used in breaking ponies, none of them were hard on the animal. A pony broken with kindness makes a finer and more trustworthy animal than one that has been broken through abuse. Of course, when we grew up with our ponies they needed no breaking. As we grew up to manhood, they grew up to horsehood, understanding us as well as we understood them.

These are all glad memories that I have told you, but I have one sad memory and that was when I went away to Carlisle to school and had to leave my little pony behind. I still remember how sad I was because I could not take him with me. Although I was to have the company of other little boys and girls who were going with me, I knew that I would miss him. I was only a little boy of eleven and the first part of the journey was fifty miles away from home, where we got on the boat that was to take us to the railroad station. I rode my pony for that fifty miles and there I had to say good-bye, for I was going East and thought at that time that I would never be back.

We learned to ride without saddles or bridles. We used the mane for a bridle, but as for saddle, we never thought of one. When we had learned to mount and ride, we just sprang on our pony as easily as you boys hop on a street-car. Away we would go over the prairie, over hills, among rocks and boulders, splash through creeks or race through woods. Riding was part of our life.

Our ponies were sure-footed, but now and then one would lose his footing and down both boy and pony would go. Quick as the pony was up on its feet so was the boy, just as if nothing had happened. Scattered over the prairie here and there were colonies of prairie dogs. These little creatures covered the ground with holes so thick that it was sometimes hard for our ponies to avoid going into one. If a pony's foot slipped into one of these holes, there was sure to be a spill. But even these we got used to. Like all my Sioux playmates I wore my hair streaming down my back, and during the warm weather of the summer months wore only a breech-cloth of buckskin. I was a real 'wild' little Indian.

Our ponies were hardy little fellows and knew how to take care of themselves when turned out to range. They were small but very strong. A hunter would come home with a buffalo that he had killed and dressed hung over the pony's back. The load would almost hide the little animal from view, yet oftentimes they plowed home for miles through deep snow without showing much fatigue. When turned loose they dug in the snow with their sharp little hoofs to get to the grass that had turned into hay under a covering of snow. These little ponies were very surefooted even on the ice. If a pony was running fast and came to a frozen stream, he would set his feet and skate across, never losing his balance. Where a buffalo stumbled and fell, our little ponies kept up. They were very quick in turning if in pursuit of buffalo or other horses, and it was the part of a good rider to keep his seat and take the turn with the pony. No matter if the pony fell and we were thrown clear of his body, we were supposed to be up and on his back by the time he had regained his feet. Even if we were injured, it was part of our training never to stay down. It was not with the idea of doing 'fancy' riding, but the thought of safety first was always in our mind. There could be no more dangerous place for a hunter than to lose his horse in the midst of a buffalo herd. We took falls and bumps which an untrained boy would not be able to stand. Ours was a life that called for strength, quick wit, and skill. But we were as much at home as the little fellow who sells newspapers on a busy street dodging here and there between swift-moving traffic. I believe, though, that out-door training is very valuable and that every boy should have the advantage of living a clean outdoor life.

When a pony had reached the age of two or three years without riding, it was then necessary to break him. Or when the camp had run short of ponies, it was up to the men to go out on the range to hunt for a herd of ponies and catch some for breaking. First they made ropes of buffalo hide to take with them. The hair was left on these ropes and they were soft but strong. Then each man who wanted to catch a pony had a long willow pole which had been peeled and dried until it was very light in weight. To the end of each pole there was tied the hide rope fastened so as to slide through a loop.

Now the wild horse is not an easy animal to catch. He is wary and a good runner. The horses always travel in bands and there is a scout or watcher for every band. So it is up to the Indian to outwit the pony if he is to make a capture. In the first place, the Indian knows the habits of the wild horse. Then the animal he rides knows just what to do when on the chase for wild ponies, so it is a case of man and his pony working together to get the wild pony in a trap. Sometimes the whole camp almost will turn out for a horse hunt. The scouts go out ahead of the hunters and locate a wild herd, preferably in a small valley. Then the hunters line up behind the hills at the four directions and out of sight of the horses in the valley. Some of the hunters will show themselves over the top of the hill from one of the directions, say the north. The wild ponies naturally turn in the opposite direction, or south. Finding hunters coming over the hill there, the wild herd will turn in another direction. But finding themselves hemmed in will start circling in the center of the valley following their leader.

After a while they will begin to tire, and then it is that the hunters get in their midst. Each hunter now selects a wild pony. When close enough to his capture, he puts the loop on the end of his willow pole over its head. The loop tightens and holds him fast. Now begins the task of getting the tame pony and wild pony acquainted. Of course the tame pony is quite fresh while the wild pony is getting weary. The rope about the wild pony's neck is made into a halter and he is tied to the gentle pony's tail, the rope being long enough to pass around the shoulders of the tame pony. The two ponies being tied together in this manner must travel together. This they don't willingly do at first, but the wild pony is not long in finding out that it is much more comfortable to follow peacefully and that he is not being hurt.

Perhaps you wonder why the captured pony submits so readily. One reason is this: There is no loud yelling, no cursing and swearing, and no whipping of our ponies. No commotion is made except that made by the feet of the running animals. In the first place, the Indian is not the noisy creature that most white people think him. He is quiet and dignified about his work. He realizes the value of keeping quiet and that is one of the first lessons of the hunter. If every one began to yell and scream, the tame pony as well as the wild one would share this mood and there would be much confusion. Besides, there are no swear words in the Sioux language and no Sioux boy ever indulged in swearing and cursing. I have never seen, in all my experience at big round-ups, the white men able to do their work without terrible cursing at their animals. The white man has never learned the use of his tongue.

Another thing we never did among the Indians was to use hot irons to mark and burn our animals which the white people call branding. The first time we saw a branding ceremony we were filled with disgust. It is a pitiable sight to see three or four men sitting on top of a helpless animal holding a white-hot iron on the shivering beast until the stench of burning flesh fills the nostrils. We had no humane societies in my time, but I know that we were humane and many times were puzzled at the things that the white man did and said.

When the hunting party reached camp, the wild horses were roped and thrown. The right fore foot was tied to the left hind foot and the left fore foot to the right hind foot. When on his feet again, he was not cruelly bound, yet he was not able to strike with the fore feet nor kick with the hind feet. The next step was to convince him that he would not be hurt. His ears, mane, and back were stroked, a rope put around his neck and he was coaxed to lead. I have seen my father break many horses, and it was he who taught me that it was never necessary nor was it right to be cruel. No animal, no matter how small, but will fight back if its captor forces it to. So I learned

35

that force is not wise nor is it just. When I grew older and my father had passed away, I owned and ran a farm where I raised and trained many horses and I never forgot what he taught me.

Indian boys were all good riders. But we tried to do more than just stay with our horses as they went over all kinds of ground. We boys used to imagine we were in battle and tried to think of the many things that might happen and how we would meet them. This was to make us quick-witted and brave. In facing an enemy, we knew it was a good idea to keep out of sight as much as possible. Sitting straight up on the horse put a warrior in plain sight of the enemy. So we practiced sitting on the side of our horses while in full speed. A number of us boys would get on our ponies and go out to an open space where we had plenty of room. There we would take turns in riding up and down in front of the rest of the group while they looked on. Pretending that we were riding in front of an enemy, we would lean away over on the side of our pony out of sight of our supposed enemy. Just our knee would be over the pony's back, but our head and body would be out of sight. We would ride this way until after considerable practice we would be able to stay in this position at full speed with just our heel over the pony's back. Only a foot would be visible to the enemy, so there was not much to shoot at.

Then we trained our pony to walk or run right up to anything we wanted him to. We picked out a good-sized bush, shrub, or trunk of a tree. Our pony was trained to run up as close as he could to the object without dodging. Our pony must learn to go wherever he was told. Even if there was shooting, yelling, and great noise and much confusion, a well-trained pony would go anywhere he was told to go by his rider.

So boy and pony trained together for warfare. We grew hardy and the more we could stand the better we liked it. Although we scarcely ever fought among ourselves, still we played quite rough with one another. We often tried to see how much the other fellow would stand and we were anxious to take all the rough handling we got. None of us wanted to be quitters. We wanted to be courageous and good-tempered. We pelted each other, we wrestled, we kicked and hit each other, but all in fun. Of course, we got hurt sometimes as do all boys, but we grew so hardy in body that we did not really mind. I have had the tears come to my eyes, but I would remember my father's words, 'Son, be brave; never give up. Fight to the last, and make up your mind that you will win!' With all this physical discipline there was a mental training as well. Although I have lived many years and been in many trying situations, I have never yet struck a person in anger.

Some Indians kept just enough ponies to get along with in their moving, but others kept on hand extra ponies. Wealth in those days was gauged by the number of ponies kept. The well-to-do man had many ponies, for his tipis were larger. It took many poles for the large tipi and many horses to carry the poles. My father had a great many ponies. Every time he went on a wild-horse hunt, he caught one or more, and then we raised them too. When we were ready to move, although it required many to do so, there were always plenty of ponies besides a number that ran loose. The ponies that ran loose were usually race or war ponies. The ones that carried the tipis and poles were the packing-ponies. They were good, but not fast, runners. One time we were moving from the Snake River to the Niobrara River. I was only a little fellow, but it was my job to drive the loose horses. I rode an iron gray pony and he was a racer. He was quite young, full of life and had a tender mouth. He was not a trained animal, but just a natural racer. When ready, I started out after the loose ponies slowly. I did not care to give this racer a chance to start running with me. Now and then the ponies would stop and eat, then, when they saw me coming near, would run on ahead a short distance. They seemed to know that, though this was moving day, no one was rushing, so they played along. I was having a good time and did not notice how far behind the moving I really was. Just ahead of me was a hill. Some of the ponies reached the top of the hill and noticed the horses and caravan far ahead of them. They started to run at full speed. Soon the entire herd that I was driving was going at full speed. My pony was too much of a racer to stand this, so he began jumping here and there. He, too, was ready to go. I held him, but when we had reached the top of the hill and I saw the rest of the herd about a half mile ahead of me, I became frightened. The hill was steep, and I knew my pony would follow the rest of the herd unless I could hold him. In a few minutes he was running down that steep hill and I was unable to do a thing with him. I was only about six years of age and, although a good rider for my age, I knew I was not good enough to stay with this horse. I could picture myself falling off and his racing on without me. I was so scared I began to cry, for I was beginning to feel sorry for myself. With eyes full of tears I kept holding to my pony, pulling the bridle first to one side and then the other with all my strength. He would lunge first to one side, then the other. Again he would take a notion to stand straight up. It was beginning to take real horsemanship to stay with this fellow. But after a while we reached the rest of the herd, and then I stopped crying. It was then that I felt ashamed of myself, but I was all alone and no one saw me. I am telling this now for the first time. The next day I asked my stepmother if I could have another pony. She said that I might take the sorrel pony. He was older and, as I had ridden him before, I knew him or thought I did.

The next day of the moving I felt quite happy. The sorrel pony was satisfied to move along with a little pace and I sang the songs that I had learned from my father. In fact I became a little careless about my work. That morning there had been a little rain and this made the loose ponies want to frisk about and kick their heels in the air. I enjoyed this very much, never for a moment thinking that my pony would do the same thing. But he did — and just as we got to a high bank. So suddenly did he take a notion to jump and run that it was all unexpected. I landed on the sheer edge of this high bank. It was steep; besides, there was nothing to catch as I went down and it was a long roll before I got to the bottom. There was brush growing on this slope, but it was dry and full of stickers, so by the time I had finished my fall, I was scratched all over my body. There were cuts on my forehead, around my eyes, and on my chin. The blood trickled down my face, and when I saw this I started to cry.

One of my stepmothers saw me fall and she rode over to me. She picked me up and, when she saw me crying, she said, 'Be brave, son. You are not a girl.' When I heard her say this, it made me want to show her that I could be brave, so I started to smile through my tears.

I rode behind stepmother until we reached camp and there they were all so good to me. They washed my face, all waiting on me as if I were a hero. When I saw father that night, he looked at me, saying, 'Son, I am proud of you that you did not cry like a woman.' My stepmother was there when he said this, but not a word was said about my crying. On each little cut or scratch father put a dot of red paint. I was then all painted up like a man who had returned from war. When all in the tribe had seen me, the paint was washed off and soon after that my face was all healed. The memory of those cuts and bruises wore away, but my stepmother's kindness in not telling on me shall always be remembered. It was her own sweet way of encouraging me always to be brave.

I have told you that we rode bareback most of the time, and so we did. However, we did have saddles which I consider much more comfortable than the white man's saddle. Our saddles were made of moose hide, which is very soft when tanned. A piece of moose hide was cut so that when folded it would form an oblong square. The hair was left on the hide, which was turned so that the hair would be on the inside. This made a soft filling for this pillow-shaped saddle. The hair of the moose never mats up, but gives the saddle the feeling of being down-filled. It was not only very soft to ride on, but very light in weight. The stirrups were made of wood covered with rawhide. To the Indian the white man's saddle, with its stiff leather seat reënforced with wood and metal, seems very heavy and clumsy. They are hard on a horse's back, which is another thing the Indian thinks of. Whenever his pony's back gets wet with sweat, the saddle is taken off and carried by the rider until the animal's back is dry. The Indian saddle is of no weight to the one carrying it and can be thrown over the shoulder when walking. The white man's saddle is not only very heavy but burdensome, and I have been made sorry more than once at the sight of a poor horse's back that had suffered from the weight and discomfort of these ugly contrivances. There is another thing that an Indian rider often does to spare his horse. He will get off and walk for long distances when on long journeys in order to let his horse regain strength and become refreshed.

CHAPTER IV

HUNTING AND FISHING

I HAVE told you much about the way we played
with our bows and arrows and how we were prepared in youth to become hunters. However,
there were many lessons that could not be learned
except with actual experience. So our fathers
helped us by taking us on the chase with them.
We were told how to get close to our game and
how to butcher and to skin. There was a right
way to cut up an animal and a right way to pack
it on the pony. This way must be learned, for it
could not be done in a haphazard way. The meat

had to be dried by the women in camp, and this was very hard to do unless cut correctly.

All this was training for the boy. Just as the mothers were training the girls to be able to be good housewives, so the fathers were teaching the sons to become skillful hunters. Our parents were our only teachers. We did not go to schools and come home with a piece of paper called a diploma. But when our training was completed, we were prepared to face life.

If we were to kill a buffalo with one arrow, we must strike a vital spot — the heart. The way to do this was to get alongside of the running animal and put an arrow just back of the shoulder. If we could not catch up with the animal and found it impossible to hit this spot, the thing to do was to aim at the soft place between the hip and the end of the ribs. A good shot at this point would reach the heart. Failing in these two methods, it was best to hit the animal straight in the center of the back between the hips. This would not, of course, be fatal, but was sufficient to stop the buffalo from running farther and then he could easily be killed. If by chance the buffalo had gone over a bank, it made this kind of a shot very easy and the hunter would be almost sure to get his game.

Now the proper skinning of the buffalo was necessary if we were to get the most out of the hide, and, of course, hides were valuable and so useful that this job was done with care and skill, leaving as little meat on the hide as possible. When the skinning was done, then the butchering began. There was a very exact method in this which I learned from my father, but there are few of the young Indians of today who know how to butcher in the old way. They are learning other things these days. We cut the animal so that the large muscles would not be cut across the grain. It was the work of the women to slice the meat in thin slices or sheets and dry it. If our work was not done properly, it made it difficult for them to do their work properly. The thin slices of meat were to be hung over a pole for drying, and if the large muscles had not been cut as they should be, the meat would fall to pieces.

Packing a buffalo on a small pony was quite a piece of workmanship and had to be done in such a way as to make an evenly balanced load. First, the hide was thrown over the pony's back, with the hair next to the pony. Then the meat was placed so that one side would not weigh heavier than the other side. The rest of the hide was thrown over the meat so that if the hunter rode, as he sometimes did, the meat was protected from both the body of horse and rider and from the dust of the trip home.

A successful hunter must learn much about the nature of wild animals. Each kind of animal has its habits and manners of living, and the success of the hunter or trapper lies in acquiring knowledge of these ways. One who is in the woods or haunts of animals receives close and intimate views of their lives, and this leads to respect for them, for they have virtues and fine qualities just as people have. The Indian very seldom bothers a bear and the bear, being a very self-respecting and peaceful animal, seldom bothers a human being. The only time the Sioux killed a bear was when it intruded into camp and some person was in danger of his life or when the meat supply ran low and it was necessary to have more meat. If the Indian and the bear happened to find themselves in the same locality, the bear kept out of the way and sight of the Indian, if possible. If, on the other hand, they met, the bear would turn around and go in the opposite direction or he might make a détour and go around if that happened to be to his greater advantage. But in any case the bear would not seek trouble.

The bear is very sensitive to the presence of man or other creatures and relies upon his nose a great deal to warn him. Standing up on his hind legs, he will thrust his nose in the air and sniff in all directions. In this way he keeps apprised of the things about him. In the matter of food the bear eats everything that the Indian eats. He likes the wild turnip that we used to dig up for food. With his long claws he digs up this plant and enjoys it very much. All the wild fruit that we ate, he ate also. For meat he would catch small animals and deer. He has a very clever way of hiding if he wishes to surprise a deer. He selects a spot along the deer path and burrows into the ground a hole large enough to cover his body. He gets into the hole and carefully spreads over himself grass and leaves until he is hidden. Here he lies until the deer comes along, and out he jumps with a swish and is upon the surprised deer. Always he strikes with the left paw, for he is left-handed.

A mother bear is very wise, and if she sees that she is being pursued by a hunter, she gets her little ones away as fast as possible. With her left paw she throws a cub some distance. Picking up the other cub, she runs to the spot where the first little one has landed. She then throws the one in her arms a distance, picks up the one on the ground and runs again. Each baby stays where he lands and awaits his mother. In this way she covers the ground quite rapidly. Ordinarily the bear is a slow-moving and dignified animal, yet, when necessary, can get over the ground very fast. He makes greater speed on level ground than up hill, as his fore legs are shorter than his hind legs.

In many ways he is so much like a human that he is interesting to watch. He has a large amount of human vanity and likes to look at himself. Before we had looking-glasses, we would look at our-

selves in a clear pool of water. This the bear
does, too, and I suppose he thinks, 'Well, I'm not
such a bad-looking fellow,' for he walks away after an inspection of himself as if quite satisfied,
and as for myself I do not see why he should not
be. He is wise and clever and probably knows it.
He likes to beautify himself by painting his face
with earth mixed with water. He finds a clear
pool in which he can plainly see himself, then
takes some earth in his paw and mixes it with water until he has a paste. This he spreads on the
left side of his face, never on the right side. Then
he looks at himself in his mirror of water. If not
satisfied with his first attempt at beautifying, he
repeats his work until he has the side of his face
fixed up as he should have it. With a last look in
his mirror, away he goes on matters of personal
concern.

Another thing of interest about the bear is the
long sleep that he takes in the winter-time. He
hides himself away in some safe cave or hollow
log and sleeps through the winter when other animals are braving the storms trying to get food
enough to pull through until spring. Of course,

by spring he is quite thin, but he soon makes up for this.

There is another reason why the Indian does not like to kill a bear unless he has to. We have in the Sioux tribe what we call 'Bear dreamers.' They are the medicine men who, during their fast, have had a vision in which the bear has come to them and revealed a useful herb or article with which to cure the sick. Whenever the bear dreamer is called to attend to a sick member of the tribe, he uses whatever the bear brought to him in the vision. For instance, if the bear told the medicine man that a certain herb would be good to give to the sick person, the medicine man would get some of this herb and use it in his ritual over the patient. Ever after the medicine man would feel indebted to the bear for his helpfulness and kindness. In this way the bear becomes useful to the tribe and for this the people have a deep feeling of gratitude. As all animals and all birds are useful to the Indian and share with him some of their secrets, the Indian has a friendly feeling toward all creatures. It is a feeling that he and all other things of earth are unified in nature. This is one of the reasons that the Indian has never been a wanton destroyer of wild life and wild growth. He has a respect for life that the white man does not seem to be able to conceive.

The bear is not only a powerful animal in body, but powerful in will also. He will stand and fight to the last. Though wounded, he will not run, but will die fighting. Because my father shared this spirit with the bear, he earned his name — Standing Bear. While in battle he was badly wounded, yet with blood streaming from his body, he did not give up and for this bravery earned a name of which he was ever after proud. Later on I will tell you how the Indian earns his name with some act of bravery or honor and how chiefs get their titles.

The Indian has always been noted for his power to track. This power to tell at a glance the difference in animal tracks comes from close observation. One of our lessons as boys was to study with care any footprint that we came upon. Different animals make tracks that are similar. For instance, the wolf and coyote make footprints that are much alike. A baby bear and a coon will leave imprints that only a skilled eye will see a difference. In fact, the similarity in some tracks is so great that a passing glance will not suffice to tell the difference. Slight as these differences are, however, a skilled Indian will know instantly what animal made the footprints that he sees upon the ground. Not only that, but he will be able to tell whether the track is a recent one or an old one. He will also know whether the animal was running or walking. If the tracks show that they were made while the animal was running, the hunter begins to look for other tracks. He may find human tracks or he may find the tracks of other animals. At any rate, he will likely find out whether the animal was being pursued or not. All these details are interesting to the hunter, especially if he is traveling in the land of an enemy.

I remember once that our camp was thrown into some excitement when it was discovered that some enemy had come into our midst. The barking of a little dog warned the men that a stranger was near. There was snow on the ground and the tracks plainly showed that some one had come into camp. Immediately the warriors surrounded the tipis feeling sure that whoever had entered could not escape. A search was made and no one found. It was then realized that whoever had come into camp had fooled every one by his tracks. The footprints were easily followed in the snow. The escaping one had run out of the village backwards and in this way got out of sight quickly. A short distance away, he had faced about and run in the natural way, as his footprints plainly showed.

In tracking a deer we came to know that it is a very hard animal to follow, for it watches behind so closely. A deer will watch the top of the hill which it has just crossed and a wise hunter will go around the base of the hill in order to deceive the animal. If a deer is sure that it is being followed, it will run some distance, then lie down and watch for its pursuer and try to locate him before going on or before exposing itself on the brow of the next hill. When hunting, we watched the direction of the wind very closely. If we did not do this, it was very likely that our game would detect us before we did it. Nature has provided the animal with a keen sense of smell, so that it can detect the presence of man and other animals at a considerable distance. So it is necessary for a good hunter to watch the wind at all times and to make détours at times in order to creep close upon the game.

Among our tribe there is a superstition concerning the black-tail deer. It is said that if this deer becomes aware of the hunter who is about to aim at it, the animal can deflect the bullets of the hunter and save itself. Many times I heard this story, then one day I had an amazing experience with this animal that puzzled me as it had other hunters. A friend and myself were hunting on horseback. The wind being right, we came close upon a black-tail deer before it saw us. I quickly dismounted to shoot while my companion held the reins of my horse. The deer did not run, but stood looking at me as I aimed, wagging its tail steadily back and forth. With every assurance of getting my game I fired. To my astonishment the deer stood still and looked intently at me. I was a good marksman, the animal was only a

THE DEER DID NOT RUN, BUT STOOD LOOKING AT ME

short distance from me, and fully exposed, yet my shot had gone astray. Seven times I shot at this animal, missing every time, the deer never moving. The seventh bullet was my last and I could shoot no more. My ammunition was gone, and there the deer and I stood looking at each other. So close were we that I could see its lips twitching. It pawed the earth once or twice with its front hoof, then dashed away. My friend accused me of being nervous, but I am not a nervous person. When I reached home, I got some more ammunition and tried out my gun. It was in perfect working order. According to my tribespeople the prairie dog and the prairie chicken both have the power to keep a hunter from hitting them.

The white man has a lodge which he calls the 'Elk Lodge.' But I often wonder if those who use the name of this proud animal know much about him. Today most of the wild animals are like the Indian — not living a natural life. But I remember when this fine animal lived an undisturbed life and was not being driven desperately here and there by the white man and his cruel and noisy gun. There was in those days peace for the Indian and for the animal, but those days are now gone. In his native state the elk has a very proud and independent manner. He walks about among his herd as if there is nothing in the sky nor on the earth that is his equal. And the others of the herd seem to think so too. Even when feeding, he never seems to forget his dignity. With every mouthful of food, up goes his head as he watches over his herd. The elk has a peculiar whistle, and whenever he wishes to get together a straying herd, he gives this whistle and all will run to him. When the herd is again clustered about him, he walks away contentedly, all the females jostling and pushing one another to get next to him. There is no doubt as to his position as leader of his herd. Sometimes two of these leaders of herds meet, and then there is fighting. If their immense horns become locked, there is no way in which they can pull apart. Both elks must die.

The Sioux make excellent bows of the elk horns. The horn is boiled until soft, then split into shape. The pieces are joined together at notches and wound with the cord of the buffalo neck. The neck cord of the buffalo is stronger than any sinew or rawhide thong or rope that we could make. It is much stronger than the neck cord of the deer or elk, so, if we wanted to put anything together for great strength, we used the neck cord of the buffalo. This cord contains a natural glue. The article that was to be joined was wound while the cord was raw or wet. When dry, the cord had glued itself so that it never came off. Things put together in this way were stronger than if nailed. I noticed when in England that the workmen who built scaffolds tied their lumber together with rawhide in much the same manner that we used the buffalo neck cord.

The hide of the elk is very strong, so we used it for wearing apparel, such as moccasins or leggins, but never for tipis. Deer hide when tanned is soft and pliable and also durable enough for tipis. Because of its pliability, deer hide was used mostly for women's and children's dresses, being white and soft as a velvet fabric. However, the elk provided teeth for decoration on the clothing. From every elk we saved two teeth and used these on dresses and shirts long before the Elk Clubman used them for a watch-charm. A woman who could afford a dress trimmed with elk teeth was considered very beautifully and expensively dressed.

For decorative purposes the fur of the otter was greatly favored by the Sioux. The young men especially liked it for its richness and softness. They made long strips of it to wind around their hair braids. If a young man owned a quiver for his bow and arrows of the otter fur, he displayed it on all dress occasions or ceremonies. It added a great deal to the expensiveness of his regalia.

We seldom saw the otter in the summer-time, but in the winter he is out in considerable numbers and much more lively and playful than in the summer. He is not a fast runner, but has a way of combining running and sliding in order to make speed if he is being pursued. He can flip himself over on his back and slide over the snow at a good pace. In shape he has a long body and short legs. He is a good swimmer, but makes more speed on land, where he can throw himself on his back for a swift slide.

The coon is an animal which the Sioux hunted also for its fur. It was a favorite along with the otter and the beaver. If a coon happened to be making his home in a tree, it was rather easy to catch him, but he had another home where he was hard to reach. The entrance to this home was under water. From the bank under the stream he burrowed up above the water-line to his den. Foxes and other animals could not reach him here, so he was safe. The coon can do something that no other animal can do, and that is walk, trot, or gallop on the bed of a stream under water just as any other animal does on land. All other animals must swim when in the water. The tail of the coon is striped with yellow and made a pretty decoration to put around the neck of a pony. We tied the tail on with a buckskin string dyed yellow. The Indian's name for the coon was 'spotted face' on account of the stripes across his face. In the winter-time his tracks could be seen in the snow leading to the hole in the ice through which he went to his burrow in the river-bank.

An animal that we observed a good deal was

61

the beaver. We noticed that, wherever there were beaver and turtles, there was plenty of water, and that if the beaver left a stream, it would not be long before the stream went dry. Little animals like this told us many things, so we watched them. The dams that the beaver builds are great things. They are built so perfectly that they do not wash away, as do the white man's dams, which sometimes go to pieces and do lots of damage. The beaver starts his dam by cutting good-sized timbers and placing them deep in the mud like piles. Then limbs of trees are laced in and out, showing that the beaver puts in an immense amount of work on a single dam. Cutting down large trees and dragging them to the water is a dangerous job, but never does a workman get killed at his labor. Whatever their system, it is a good one. Sometimes we discovered that a beaver colony had moved to another creek, but we never saw a beaver on land, nor did we ever catch a colony of these animals on the march moving their town site. That was something of a mystery to us; also the fact that as sure as the beaver moved, the stream that they left would go dry.

We admired the beaver, for he is very industrious. Just the same he likes to play. They like to splash water over each other with their tails. Then they build slides of earth and mud, and carry water up on them with their tails until the slope is smooth and shiny. When the game is going big, even the old ones join the young ones, and everybody has a good time. I have seen many wild animals fight, but I have never seen one beaver battle with another one, so I take it that they are inclined to be peaceful. The beaver ponds were always beautiful spots, fresh and green, and we were sure to see many other kinds of animals lingering about that liked the water and the trees. The meat of the beaver is quite good, the tail being entirely of fat. When cooked, this tail tastes something like cheese, and we ate it with our lean meat like bread.

The turtles which we caught out of the beaver pond made a good food, so we boys often went fishing for turtles. First we looked for them along the banks. If we did not find them there, we went into the water for them, either wading or swimming. Turtles like sun baths, so we slipped along quietly, hoping to catch sight of them lying in the sand. Maybe a log extended from the water to the shore and a whole row of turtles would be on it enjoying the sun. We seldom caught them, however, for as soon as they heard us, they would flop off into the water one by one. We would then have to go into the water, possibly up to our necks, and walk around feeling for them with our feet. Pretty soon our feet would touch the slippery back of a turtle. Down we dived and threw him out on the bank, where one of the boys turned him over on his back. There he lay helpless until we were ready to start home. Next day mother had turtle soup for dinner.

Once in a while we found one of these fellows that was too large for one of us to get on shore. Then we called for help, and several of us would manage to drag our turtle to the bank and turn him over on his back. If one of these big fellows took a notion to move about while we were on his back, we just stood still and moved about with him. This we thought was lots of fun. We enjoyed being in the water and were all good swimmers. Swimming and riding were our chief sports.

The Sioux name for the turtle is 'water-car-rier,' for the reason that when a turtle left a pond or stream that body of water became dry as if they took the water with them. Great numbers of these water-loving animals moved over the land in changing their places of living, yet like the beaver we never saw them on the march. It would have been interesting to see them travel-ing, for they often covered rough country, climb-ing logs and even banks of considerable height. They have long claws and they use these for climbing. The slightest noise will arouse them, though, and I think by this sense they are most protected.

Happy days were our fishing days. When we went fishing, we did not have fine reels and rods and lines already made up for us like the white boy. But we caught the fish just as easily as we caught the turtles. Not having all these things, we had to be resourceful. If we wanted to catch fish, we had to find some way to do so or go with-out. I assure you, though, that we did not go without our fish, but some days got a good catch to roast by a fire or take home to mother. Perhaps some boy in camp would decide it was a good day to go fishing and would call to the other boys playing about the tipis, and soon there would be a crowd of us on our way to the fishing pools. But we had to get ready on the way. We started empty-handed and had to get our tackle before we got to the creek. First we went to our ponies and got some of the longest hairs from his tail. For bait we had a piece of buffalo meat. Fish will not notice cooked meat, so, of course, our bait was raw. Also fish are attracted to red, so we gathered along our way some red berries, perhaps the buds of the wild rose. By throwing one of these into the water, we would soon find out if there were any fish there. We tested for fish in this way until we found a spot where the fish were before using our buffalo meat. When ready, we tied a piece of meat to the end of our horsehair line, and when a fish had swallowed the piece of meat, he was quickly thrown on the bank. We landed him with a jerk by throwing him to our right side if he was on the left side when caught. If he was on the right when in the water, we threw him to our left.

But suppose we got down to the river without a fishing line. We then looked about for a long willow pole. The end that was slim and limber we looped over, making a hoop just big enough to catch a fair-sized fish. We put our looped end down into the water, and soon the little fishes were swimming through it. These we did not want, but pretty soon along would come a big fellow and he would try to go through the loop. With a quick motion we would jerk up our pole and the fish would land on the bank. When we had all the fish we wanted to carry home, we got a stick with a forked branch at one end. On this we strung our fish to take home.

In our hunts we learned much of the habits of birds as well as animals. We watched them closely, for they taught us many things. Birds are graceful beings, and the Indian loves beauty in movement. In his dances the Indian is highly imitative, and many of his steps he gets from the birds. Besides, they have virtues such as industry, kindness, affection, and pride. They have also keen senses that the Indian admires.

On the plains of South Dakota there were in

my boyhood many prairie chickens. They were fine to eat, and when we picked them, we saved the wing feathers for our arrows. These birds.began to travel south with the cold weather, but there were always a few that lingered behind until after snow fell. They would feed on buffalo berries and on the rosebuds that ripened in the fall. Now, some people may think that human beings were the first to dance, but I do not think so. I believe that the birds danced first. I also believe that they appreciate time and rhythm. I have seen the prairie chickens hold dances as orderly and as well-organized as I have seen humans hold. The dance of the prairie chicken is given at daybreak. A great number of these birds will assemble and form a circle with the leader in the center. Then the circle begins moving to the right, every bird stepping at the same time and the same speed in motion. Their time is so perfect that even if it were performed in silence, it would be wonderful to look at. But the marvelous thing is that every bird makes a sound in his throat that is something like the double beat of the tom-tom. In this, too, the birds keep exact

time, so that there are no jarring or conflicting
noises, but a steady rhythmic tone. Every bird
carries a rattle — his tail. The feathers of the
tail are rubbed together in such a way as to make
a sound like a small rattle. Again the time is
kept with the tails all moving at the same time in
the same way. With feet, voices, and tails moving at the same time, it makes a great sight to see
a hundred or more birds performing. Perhaps
the Indian is more easily touched and thrilled at
such sights as these than the white man — I do
not know. But surely these dances are conducted
with a dignity unknown to our modern young
people and their silly Charlestons and Blackbot-
toms. I am a man of the theater and have been
for many years, but I would rather see this dance
today than any vaudeville number I have ever
seen. To me there is a lesson in the fact that these
birds rise early in the morning and dance with
the rising sun. That is the logical time for creatures of the day to start their activities: not
dance all night and go to bed when the sun is rising. Without doubt the prairie chickens enjoy
these early morning dances that they perform,

for if they discover that some one is watching them, they fly away, showing plainly that they are not pleased at being disturbed. The prairie chicken, the meadowlark, and the crow are birds that make sounds that can be interpreted into Sioux words. We Sioux knew, of course, that birds and animals had a way of talking to one another just as we did. We knew, too, that the animals and birds came and talked to our medicine men. Our legends tell of the time when bird and animal life communicated with man.

We boys were quite fond of the eggs of the prairie chicken, but if we went hunting, we usually looked for the male and not the female bird. He was a guard for the nest, and if we got close would set up a big racket to scare us away.

The duck is a bird that means a good deal to the Sioux people. I told you about the bear dreamer and how the bear helped the Sioux by telling the medicine men about a valuable herb that would cure the sick. So we have a duck dreamer. Long ago, while a medicine man fasted, the duck came to him in a vision and told him about a plant that grew only in the water. The

70

root of this plant is good for those who have nervous troubles, and we all use it to this day. The duck also showed the Sioux how to dig for the lily roots that grow in ponds. The women of the tribe boil these roots, which are something like sweet potatoes and are very nourishing. In some of our most sacred and religious ceremonies we use the beautiful green breast of the duck in this way, showing our thankfulness to this bird. On the peace pipe there is a bit of the neck feathers, and in the confirmation ceremony a duck feather is worn with the eagle feather which is put on the head of the one being confirmed. The duck is considered very wise for his knowledge of the air and of the water as well.

The duck never flies at night, but sleeps close to the banks of lakes and streams. My father used to tell me that, if the warriors heard ducks flying at night, they kept a watch for enemies, for they would only be flying if disturbed. Every sound, whether by night or by day, had a meaning for the Sioux warrior. How much we relied on our furred and feathered friends!

Our people admired the owl and liked to wear

71

his feathers. It was the ability of the owl to see at night and catch its prey in the dark that made the Indian admire this bird. The owl hunts only at night preying upon mice, and quick as mice are, the owl is much quicker. The Sioux have a society or lodge called the Owl Lodge, the members all wearing caps covered with owl feathers. The Indian's faith is great, and he believes that by wearing the owl feathers and thus showing his respect for nature, he will be favored by nature by having his own powers of sight increased. It is a fact that the vision of the members of the Owl Lodge was exceedingly keen. These men of the lodge feel that they are rewarded for their appreciation of the owl. The Indian has always wanted and sought the powers possessed by birds and animals and which have been denied him. So, farther back in history than we can remember, the Indian formed societies and lodges named after birds and animals. Then he strove to acquire their powers. In cultivating this wish, he became very sensitive to all his surroundings. He became alive and alert and living was a joy to him.

Warriors who have been brave in war are sometimes allowed to wear a cap of owl feathers as a mark of their bravery. Or a scout who had risked his life to get information would be honored by being allowed to wear a cap of owl feathers.

One day a Sioux scout reported that he had seen a smoke. Now a scout does not expose himself out on an open plain, but goes where he can secrete himself and watch without being seen. So this scout went to a wood and hid himself behind a large cottonwood tree. As evening drew near, he heard the cry of an owl close by. Listening, he soon realized that the sound was coming nearer. The shadows were growing, but still he could see some distance ahead. Soon the figure of a man appeared, and it was he that was hooting and not an owl. This aroused the suspicion of the Sioux scout, as he could not yet tell whether the approaching man was friend or enemy. Closer the man came, hooting like an owl, until the scout could see that he was an enemy Indian trying to steal into the Sioux camp, which was some distance away in the woods. The scout was not pleased at meeting this enemy alone and was wishing that some of his friends were with him. However, he was brave and stood his ground. When the enemy came close to the tree behind which the scout was hidden, the Sioux sprang out so suddenly and seized the enemy so quickly that the intruder fell in a faint. The scout then called for some friends and with their help carried the enemy to the camp and revived him. In sign language he was told to speak the truth and tell whether he was alone or leading a band. If he spoke truthfully, he would not be injured, but if he was found to be lying, he would receive hard punishment. He promised to tell the truth. The captive Indian said that he was not leading a band, but was alone. His band was several days' travel away. He explained that he had not come to kill, but that he was afoot and needed a horse and had only come to see if he could make away with one. The Sioux were convinced that their enemy was telling the truth and for this they decided to give him a horse. Since he had not come to kill, they would show him kindness in his want. He was given a horse and told to go back to his band. This he did and rode away. This is an instance showing that the Sioux were not the cruel and revengeful tribe that white man's history says he is. There are many stories of my tribe that show that they were kind to their captives and killed only when necessary to safeguard themselves. No Sioux ever took advantage of a luckless person.

This happening shows that they are not unfair even to one who is not a friend: One day a band of Sioux ran across a lone enemy. The enemy, seeing himself faced by a number of warriors, looked about for a safe direction to run. Being not far from the village of the Sioux, he decided to run for the chief's tipi. The tipi of the chief can be easily distinguished, as it is larger than the rest of the tipis and stands a little apart from the circle. Straight into the chief's home ran the fellow, with the band of warriors right behind him. When the enemy reached the door of the tipi, he walked in and quietly seated himself while the pursuing Indians stopped outside. A white man running unceremoniously into a home would likely kneel down and pray to be spared or protected. But the Indian, walking in and seating himself in silence, means all that the white man would mean by imploring in speech and manner. The chief knew this Indian, who had seated himself so quietly in his tipi, was an enemy, yet he was a man seeking for help. The chief simply said to his wife, 'Prepare this man some food, for he is a long way from his home and people.' The food was placed before him and he accepted it gratefully, for he knew that the chief was treating him as a friend. In order further to impress the visitor with his good will toward him, the chief took the pipe of peace and, pointing it in the four directions and up to the sky, then down to mother earth, assured the man sitting in his tipi that he need have no fears. When the meal was finished, the visitor was given a pony and told that he would not be bothered as long as he was in Sioux territory.

The Indian, as you know, is used to being laughed at by the white people. Whenever white people see an Indian wearing some feathers, they seem to think it a funny sight, forgetting that they, too, wear feathers. Furthermore, they do not wear them with the feeling of reverence that the Indian feels. With the white people feathers are worn with the sole idea of decoration, but with the Indian it is with the hope that he may ennoble his character.

I have often noticed the famous drug-stores that have the owl as a trade-mark, advertising that they are up at night and will serve their patrons at all hours. That is a good symbol, for the owl slept during the day and worked and lived at night. But I often wonder if it has any but a commercial meaning to the white man. Now, my readers, after this when you see an Indian wearing feathers, do not laugh. Instead think of what they mean to him. Remember that the Indian has learned from the wonderful birds, and also remember that the Indian has a great love for all things that are natural. Whenever the Indian sees things in the white man that he does not understand, he does not laugh. They may seem funny to him, but he begins to wonder if there is something hidden from him. He begins to think and seek an explanation for what he cannot account for. If you will take this attitude toward the Indian, you will find that he has things to teach you of a world of which you do not know.

The white man calls the eagle the 'king of birds.' And he is, perhaps, the bird of which the Indian thinks the most. At least, the eagle symbolizes to the Indian the greatest power. In olden times the Sioux people believed that, if they killed the eagle, some bad luck would come to them or to some member of the family. Still they loved to wear his feathers, for he had such great strength and vision. He flew so high in the sky that he reached the realm of the gods and could look the world over. So the Indian wore the feathers of the eagle long before the white man came to this land. And he wore them, not to 'look nice,' but with awe and appreciation of the wonder of nature.

For many centuries before the Indian had the gun, he killed animals and birds with the bow and arrow. But the eagle was the sole creature that he had to capture. No hunter could get close enough to the eagle to shoot him with an arrow. Even his capture was so difficult that great care was taken in carrying out plans for his capture. Also there was a religious feeling toward this fine creature, so that the arrangements for the capturing and killing of this bird took the form somewhat of a ritual.

The taking of an eagle was a serious and dangerous event and several days were used in preparation. Three men were required to carry out the plans. These men went away by themselves to the haunts of the eagle. They set up their tipi and filled it with sweet-smelling sagebrush, with the exception of the space left for the fire and the altar. Upon this fragrant sage they slept at night. In the center the camp-fire was kept burning. The door of the tipi opened to the east to face the rising sun. In the back of the tipi opposite the door, an altar of earth was built marked at the four directions by four sticks to which were tied little bags of the sacred tobacco. Close to the altar a stand was erected against which rested the pipe of peace. Some fifty feet or more from the tipi was constructed a small willow hut with the door also facing the east. This custom of building with doors facing the east shows the Indian's reverence for the sun. Over the willow hut were thrown blankets, so that it was air tight. In the middle of the floor of the hut, a hole was scooped out of the ground large enough to hold a number of stones.

When the hut was finished, the man who was to catch the eagle went into it for his sweat bath. He had come with his mind purified with veneration and his body must be purified, too. It was no playing matter with this man. For three or four days he fasted and took the sweats before he felt good and clean. In the mean time the other two companions and helpers had gone close to the place where the eagle was known to live. Here they dug a hole large enough to hold a man's body in a sitting position. While digging the hole, they carried away the earth in their blankets, taking it some distance from the hole. They poured it here and there, so that it would resemble anthills. The eagle is so watchful and suspicious that it was necessary to do this in order not to attract his attention and cause him to suspect an enemy's presence. While the men worked around this hole, they were careful to walk on the grass and not make tracks in the soil.

These tracks the eagle would notice if made in the earth and he must be deceived in every way. After the earth had been carefully distributed, the top of the hole was concealed with grass and shrubs. It was then ready for the man who had purified himself with the sweat baths. His two helpers assisted him into the holes and covered him up so that even an eagle's eye would not detect anything unusual. All this concealing of the man was done before the break of day.

In olden times the catcher of the eagle would take into the hole with him his bow and arrow, but in my day a firing weapon of some kind was generally used. This was a brave man's game and none but a brave man would attempt it. Just before the helpers went away, they placed a piece of meat on top of the hole. It was held down by a buckskin thong. This meat would not only be smelled by the eagle, but by animals such as coyotes, wolves, or bears. Probably they would come before the eagle got there, so it was a dangerous position for the man to be in. When once seated in the hole, the catcher must be very quiet and hold his nerve, for he was now alone.

His helpers had gone away, leaving him to face whatever might happen. They dare not stay around him, for then no game would approach. Here he must wait for hours without food and water and in the utmost quiet. It was at the best a trying position.

When the eagle smelled the meat, he began circling high in the air, his eye ever looking for enemies. Closer and closer he circled, and at the sight of him the smaller animals scurried out of sight, for they all feared him. When all looked safe, the eagle lighted near the piece of meat. Still as a statue he would stand, turning his head this way and that, looking and listening. His ears were keen, just as his eyes were, and the hunter must make no sound. When satisfied that nothing was near that might be harmful, he walked closer to the meat. Again he would look and listen and at last make an attempt to pick it up. He would try to fly up with it, but of course the helpers had seen to it that it was securely fastened. So there the eagle stood probably reflecting on the situation.

Now was the time for the hunter to get his

prize. Reaching up very quietly and easily, the man in the hole caught the eagle's leg just above the foot. If this was done softly and gently, the eagle would not move. Perhaps he was held by curiosity or perhaps by fear, but as long as no abrupt movement was made, there was no struggle on the part of the eagle. The hunter tightened his hold on the eagle's leg and slowly slid his hand up above the feather-line on the thigh. Now he had a firm hold of the eagle, and slowly and quietly began to draw him down into the hole. Still there was no opposition from the eagle. The hunter, raising his free hand, deftly wrung the eagle's neck and placing a stake across its neck held it there until he was sure the bird was dead. Then he took his catch to the tipi which his two helpers had helped him set up.

The body of the eagle was laid on a white buckskin placed at the head of the altar. Then over its body the pipe was pointed to the north, south, east, and west, lifted to the sky above and lastly down to mother earth. The head of the eagle, from which the feathers had been plucked, was painted red to the neck, and in the mouth was placed a bit of meat that had been prepared for food. This was all done with the idea of showing the Great Mystery that the life He had created was respected and to show in a humble way that the Indian was thankful for all the gifts that Nature had given him. So just for one eagle the Indian was willing to purify himself and endure hardship. When the beautiful feathers had been plucked, the body of the eagle was carried back to the place where he was caught. It was left lying on the beautiful white buckskin with its head toward the east. There it was consigned to the Great Mystery who takes care of all things.

One curious thing about the eagle is that its dead body is never found. It is not known that any one in our tribe ever found even the feathers of an eagle, though our hunters often looked for them.

There is a language of feathers for the Indian. The way and the number of eagle quills that a warrior wears on his head have a meaning. He must, of course, be honest in his wearing of them, and cannot, for instance, paint his quills red if he has not suffered a wound at the hand of the enemy.

There are four ways in which the brave wears the eagle feather, each way denoting how he has met the enemy. The bravest warrior, who has gone ahead of the rest and led the way or faced the enemy and either touched him or killed him, wears a feather straight up at the back of his head. The next bravest man wears his feather pointing sideways to the right from the back of his head. The third bravest man wears his feather in the same way as the second bravest, only it points to the left side. The fourth bravest man wears his feather hanging straight down his back. A red stripe straight across the quill meant that the man wearing it had been wounded once by the enemy. Sometimes a warrior who had been on many war parties wore two and three or even four stripes on his feather. A brave man who had been surrounded by the enemy and had fought his way out wore a very pretty decoration on the side of his head. It was made of a tuft of feathers, from the center of which there hung a buckskin string, to the end of which there was tied a single eagle feather. At large social gatherings and council meetings the warriors all wore their various decorations, and every one knew what deeds of bravery each man had performed by looking at the decorations. A lot of thrilling stories were told without any speech-making. Also it was quite the custom at gatherings for the braves to relate their war exploits in action and in mimicry. This some of the warriors could do very dramatically.

The war shield of the Sioux is a very interesting article of warfare. They can scarcely be found today, for there were not a great many made even in the warring days of the Sioux. When the braves of our tribe went out to battle with the foe, they put most of their faith in a good bow and arrow. The shield was made of buffalo hide which was thoroughly toughened and shrunk with heat. First a hole was dug and a cottonwood fire built in it. When only the hot embers were left, a green buffalo hide was spread over the hole just close enough to get the heat from the coals. In a short time the hide would begin to shrink, so it was held down around the edges with stones. Now and then a little water was thrown over the coals to form steam. Slowly the hide shrunk and thickened. Smaller and smaller it grew until it was so thick and tough that no arrow could pierce it. The skin was then taken off the heat and cut into the proper shape and size. It was covered with buckskin and two handles put on it for the arm of the warrior. It was then decorated with the designs of the Sioux either by the medicine man or the warrior himself. In either case the symbols or drawings that were painted on the shield were equal in sense to a motto which might read, 'Your faith will keep you safe.' After the painting was done, eagle feathers were fastened on with dyed buckskin strings. When the warring days of the Sioux were over, many of these shields were carried to the mountain-tops as was the body of the eagle and left there to go slowly back to the elements.

Then the Sioux warrior had a banner which was sometimes carried to war. It was a pole decorated from top to bottom with eagle feathers which floated in the breeze as it was carried. Then we had our flag. Yes, the Indian had a flag long before the white man came! It was a fine thing to look at and every Indian was proud of it. The flag of the Sioux was a pole with a crook at the top like a staff. This pole was wrapped in otter skin and decorated with eagle feathers. It was a sacred symbol to the tribe and could only be made in the lodge. Sometimes it was given to a young warrior who was going into the greatest danger and probably never would come back to his people.

The women of the Sioux tribe wore only the soft downy feathers of the eagle. This decoration is only permissible when a woman has had the confirmation ceremony performed over her. It is then worn tied to the hair on the left side. For a Sioux woman to wear one of these decorations is a mark of distinction and places her in a high position in the tribe. These white and dainty feathers of the eagle are also used in the dancing wands which the corn dancers wear in the confirmation ceremony. Sometimes these soft feathers are dyed in beautiful colors and made into tassels or pendants.

Crazy Horse, who is said to have been one of

the greatest of military geniuses and surely the greatest warrior of the Sioux tribe, always wore a hawk at the side of his head. He was as sure and swift as the hawk himself. The hawk soars above a flock of birds and, darting down in their midst, sends a luckless bird to the ground. The hawk may be cruel, but he is feared by most birds. Whether the medicine man told Crazy Horse to wear the hawk, I do not know, but at any rate he was as fearless as the hawk.

So it is not true that only the chiefs wear the large showy head-dresses or war-bonnets made of the eagle feathers. Any hunter who was brave enough to capture an eagle was entitled to wear a head-dress of eagle feathers. But some of the greatest warriors and chiefs chose to wear simpler decorations.

One of the marks of a fine and complete regalia with the Sioux was a fan of eagle feathers. I once possessed one that was very beautifully put together with dyed porcupine quills and a beaded handle.

When we boys played about the camp, we noticed that the blackbirds were great friends of our ponies and that flocks of them followed the animals while they grazed. The ponies stirred up the grass as they walked about disturbing the grasshoppers and other insects upon which the birds fed. We boys would shoot at the birds, the horses never paying any attention to us.

I remember, however, one day when I started a small riot in camp by accidentally hitting a pony. It was moving day and the entire camp was packing and breaking up. My job was to take the pins out of our tipi when ready to move and to put them up for mother when we stopped at a new camp. When the tipi was up, mother would lift me in her arms so that I could reach the height where the first pin was placed. While mother held me, I placed the first pin, then used it to step on as you do the rung of a ladder while I put in the next one above. So up I went with each pin until all were in, then I climbed down. This day I had helped mother all I could and was playing about shooting at the blackbirds. One of my arrows bounced off the ground and struck a pony in the tender part of the jaw. The pony was all packed with household goods and had been peacefully grazing. When suddenly startled with the blow from the arrow, he began lunging about. This caused the pack to fall off, scattering things all over the ground. This frightened the animal, and he started to run. Other animals became frightened at the commotion and began to run also.

Soon the entire camp was in a state of excitement. Camp goods were strewn over the ground. Horses shied or jerked at their tethers, while others were running loose. Women ran here and there, men shouted, and finally there was disorder everywhere. Though I was not guilty of any intentional wrongdoing, I got on my pony and rode away as fast as I could go. I was thoroughly frightened at what I had done and faster and faster I went, urging my pony with a switch that I carried. Not until I went over a hill and out of sight did I slacken my pace and look around. No one was following me, so I stopped a moment to reflect. Finally I went back to the top of the hill and peeped over. No one seemed to be looking for me, for everyone was busy bringing about order or going ahead with preparations for moving. Still I lingered out of sight over the top of the hill until the camp was on the march. Then I joined my parents in the moving line. I still expected to be scolded for my carelessness, but not a word was ever said to me, though I knew that my folks were fully aware that I was to blame for this uproar. I knew that a scolding would be the extent of my punishment, yet I ran away with as much fright as a boy would who expected a good thrashing.

I am glad to say that I learned a good lesson that day, for deep within I resolved never to be so careless again. Little as I was, perhaps six or seven years of age, I realized that I had done something which I must not do again. To this day I look back upon my childhood and say with pride that, in all the days spent with my mother and father, never did I feel the sting and humiliation of a blow from their hands. I know that no white boy lives who reveres the memory of father and mother more than I do. Though they were full-blooded Indians, they were good and wise and worthy of my tenderest thoughts.

CHAPTER V

PLANTS, TREES, AND HERBS

THE world of animal and bird contributed much to the comfort and welfare of the Indian, but so did plant, tree, and herb. The Indian overlooked nothing that might be of service to him. He went deep into the possibilities of all plant life. Simple plants which the white man calls weeds became things of value to the Indian. Some provided a wholesome food, while others were brewed into health-restoring medicines. The white man takes bitter drugs, and pays good prices to another man to give them to him, whereas if he was content to live simply as the Indian does, he probably would have better health. But he disdains Nature and pays for it in hard-earned dollars. Our medicine men were poor, but the white man's medicine men are rich.

Now, one of the most useful of trees to the Sioux was the cottonwood. This tree was used from its top to its roots and from its bark to its heart. The bark was used for all fires where coals were needed. This bark was, in fact, as good as the coal we now use in our stoves. The flame burned without sparks and sputtering, so there was no danger of the tipi catching fire, though in the winter the fire burned all night while the family slept. When the flames had gone down, the coals burned with a steady, penetrating glow that kept the tipi well warmed. Only cottonwood bark was used for heating our paints and for tanning our hides.

Next to the outer bark of the tree was a thin juicy layer of bark, and this we children chewed, as it was sweet and tasty. For all ceremonial purposes the cottonwood was favored. Out of it were made the tripods for sacred articles to hand on, and the cross in the sun dance was made of a cottonwood tree. In the winter, when the snow had covered the grass, a cottonwood tree was

cut down and our ponies driven over to feed on
its bark. All night these little ponies chewed
busily and by morning the branches of the tree
would be stripped of bark. Then the tree was
ready to be cut up into firewood. The ponies
grew fat on this bark, and it was a change of diet
for them, although they were industrious and
could always find plenty of grass by digging
through the snow with their feet.

Cottonwood does not split easily, and when
dry is very light in weight. For this reason we
made saddles out of it lined with buffalo hide.
Neither does the wood bend easily, so we generally used a soft wood like elm for the stirrups.
Our spinning-tops we made of the cottonwood,
for we spun them on the hard ground or even on
the ice in the wintertime and they never chipped
nor cracked. It seems rather strange, but the
roots of this tree are very light and spongy and
will float on the water. We boys often used
a piece of the root to keep us afloat if we were
crossing a wide stream. The girls made dolls of
this part of the tree also. Many times they found
pieces just right in size and already shaped with

arms and legs so that they needed little forming to make a good doll. The girls made dresses of buckskin for their dolls, then painted the face and hair. When completed and dressed up in a painted and beaded buckskin dress, some of these dolls were very pretty.

In the springtime the cottonwood tree bears large clusters of pods which in late summer break open and a fine white cotton goes floating about in the air. This fleecy material we gathered to fill our soft buckskin pillows.

Another tree which we found almost as useful as the cottonwood was the cedar — the tree that the white people call evergreen. Whenever we boys did not feel well, grandmother or mother would make us a tea of cedar leaves which were kept in a rawhide bag hanging in the tipi. Sometimes a few leaves of the sagebrush would be mixed with the cedar leaves. This tea tasted bitter, but we drank it whenever we were told to, and soon we would be out playing and feeling all right again. When a thunderstorm came up, some woman of the household would get the bag of cedar leaves and throw a handful on the coals of fire. In a moment or so the tipi would be filled with the sweet smell of the cedar smoke. When I was a little fellow I saw this done many times — for thunderstorms are frequent in South Dakota — and I wondered why. Then one day father told me something marvelous about the cedar tree. He said the cedar tree protected the Sioux people and their tipis from lightning. This tree has never been known to be struck with lightning, and he warned me that, if ever caught away from home in a thunderstorm, to ride for a cedar tree and stay under it with my pony until the storm was over. The old Sioux still tell about the days when they were safe from lightning, but now that they live in the white man's tents several of them have been killed.

Another thing we found about the cedar tree was that it never was attacked by worms. Other trees were often spoiled by insects, but the cedar tree was always healthy. Perhaps this is the reason, as well as for its sweet odor, that the white man uses it for clothes chests. We made our flutes of cedar wood, but seldom used it for bows. It had a very good spring, but when it broke it could not be fixed, for it always broke in many pieces.

We needed a light, resonant wood for our drum bands or cases, so the elm wood provided us with this kind of wood. It was easy to bend into shape and easy to cut into thin strips. When we got to farming, then we used the elm more. One day I made a discovery. While some distance away from home, I broke the ridgepole on my wagon. In place of the broken ridgepole, I put one of the elm. I was hoping that my repair job would last until I got home, then I could get a stronger wood. Through the end of the ridgepole I bored a hole into which fitted an iron bolt, and I felt that this iron would split the soft wood. However, after a few days I found that the section of wood through which the bolt passed had worn hard and smooth. This surprised me, so I told others of it, and after that elm was used a good deal on the farm.

The box elder was the first wood used for pipestems. The heart of this tree is soft and pithy. A branch of elder was selected for the pipestem. The pithy center was burned out by using burning sticks and running them down through the center of the pithy branch. It burned quickly and soon there was a nice pipestem. After we got wire, we made pipestems of the ash wood instead of the box elder. Like the maple tree the elder runs a sweet sap. Out of notches cut in the tree the sap ran, and this we caught and drank, but never tried to make sugar of it. The first sugar we saw was brought to us by the white man. The elder has its peculiarity like most other woods. Wherever it forked, it would twist, making it so strong that it would not split. These forks were just what we needed for bracing the tipi poles when it was windy and the poles needed strengthening. The popguns of the boys were all made of elder on account of being easy to bore through.

Now the white people have many ways of learning about plants. They test for poisons and food properties in ways that the Indian did not know about. If a white man thinks a plant is poison, he tests it on his friend the animal. No wonder the animals came to our medicine men and told them what herbs and plants were good to eat, pointed out those that were poison and told us where to find those that would cure us when sick. Then there were plants that furnished us with beautiful and fast-colored dyes. With these bright colors we dyed our porcupine quills, buckskins, feathers, and painted interesting things on our tipis.

In the springtime the young grapevine came up in profusion. These leaves with some of the grapes the women gathered and put all together in a rawhide bag. The leaves were torn apart and the grapes crushed and all thoroughly mixed together. This made a very pretty red color, and the article to be dyed red was put into the mixture and left there until it had taken up the color. Porcupine quills dyed in this way keep their color for years on moccasins that have very hard wear.

I remember a slender plant that grew on a stalk about two or three feet high. This plant had a thorn that made it unpleasant to our ponies, so we boys called it 'Enemy leg.' We often played that it was our enemy and we would run our ponies up to it as close as we could. This plant had a purplish bloom that was crushed up to make yellow dyes of various shades. Into this fluid we dipped our arrows, feathers, or other objects that we wanted to be yellow in color.

I wonder if little boys have always liked to chew gum? You boys go to the store and buy a package of gum all wrapped up in pretty paper, but we boys had to manufacture our gum. We gathered a weed that grew on the plains and hills of my home land. We broke the leaves of this plant and out flowed a white sticky substance. We put each bit into our mouths until we had enough to chew. This gum had a nice flavor and we liked it, for it did not crumble up like pine gum.

There were plants which we used only for their perfumes. Some of these plants throw their perfume for a distance away and the air would be sweet and delightful. The sweetgrass is one of these plants that one can smell for a long way off, and we loved to gather it and braid chains of it to wear about our necks. The brave loved perfume as well as any woman, and if he went calling on a sweetheart he wound chains of fragrant plants around his neck and also around the neck of his horse or tied some to the tail of his animal. A small running vine grew along the creeks that was almost as fragrant as the sweetgrass. This we gathered to wear or hang in the tipis. Then there was a plant that held its fragrance long after it had dried, and this the women put in little bags to hang about their necks.

Our food plants were numerous. We gathered plants that grew wild for us, and which you cultivate now and call by such names as cauliflower, potatoes, and turnips. We also had some corn, but did not raise it as did other tribes. Mother often flavored soup with a little plant that was quite common about our home, but I cannot give you the name for it in English.

Most of our medicine plants were known only to the medicine men, but we had some that we used ourselves, as the cedar and sagebrush tea. Then there was also a tea made from the bark of the chokecherry. The muskrat ate a root that grew in the swamps, so our name for it translated into English is 'muskrats' food.' This root the Sioux used for nervousness, and the women often carried a piece of it tied around their necks to have it ready to offer to anyone who felt nervous and upset. When our horses were troubled with distemper, we made a tea of a plant that grew on the plains. We poured this tea down the horse's throat, for no horse would drink it willingly. However, it was a good remedy and always helped them.

Long ago the wolf came to the medicine man and told him how to use the tobacco plant. The wolf digs into the earth and is wise about the things that grow up from the soil, so he told the medicine man that if the tobacco plant was burned in the tipi, it would keep away disease and purify the air. The women threw the leaves of this plant on the fire and the smoke would rise up and fill the tipi. Long before pipes had been invented, the men would draw coals from the fire and sprinkle the dried leaves over the coals. As the smoke arose, they covered their heads with their blankets and bent over the coals so they could breathe in the smoke. A little later, men learned to smoke another way. Lying on the ground they drew the smoke into the mouth

103

through a hollow reed. The next pipe was more convenient, for it was the small leg bone of the deer hollowed out. A piece of charcoal was put in one end of the bone and on this the tobacco. It was carried in the mouth and smoked like a cigar. This bone pipe was carried by the smoker just as the men today carry their pipes, only in those days there were no pockets. A ring was notched around the middle of the bone and a buckskin string tied to it. The other end of the string was tied to the man's belt. When an Indian camped for the night and he had a pony that might stray away, he put this bone pipe to the end of the pony's tether. Then he buried the bone pipe deep enough in the ground to hold the pony. In the morning he took his pipe from the earth, cleaned it off, and it was as good as ever, while the pony was there to start the day's journey.

How long men smoked without a bowl to the pipe, we do not know, but it must have been a long time. Then a medicine man had a vision in which was brought the knowledge of the pipe stone. So when the white man came among us, we were using the pipe with a bowl. This third pipe was made of a material called soapstone. The old men of the tribe tell us that it was found in this way.

The Sioux were camped on the Missouri River somewhere on the east side. The medicine man told the people of his vision and that the place where this wonderful stone lay buried in earth had been revealed to him. At once preparations were made to go to the land where this stone was to be found. There was no argument with the medicine man, no question as to where he would lead them. The Sioux believed in their medicine men. They were our wise men and we had faith just as the people in Bible days had faith in their wise men. Our medicine men were always searching for and finding things that were of benefit to us. So the entire camp moved to the place where the medicine man said the stone would be found. Flint tools were all they possessed in those days, so with these they began to dig in the earth. They came to a layer of stone, but it was not what they were looking for. The second layer of stone which they came to was still not the right kind. They continued digging and came to a third layer of stone, but still they had not found what they were searching for. Nevertheless, the digging went on. The fourth time they came to stone, it proved to be a soft red stone, and they knew that they had found what they were looking for — the stone for the pipe of peace.

Out of this stone was made the first pipe that was to become the most powerful symbol the Sioux have. The first pipes that were made were not so large as they are today, for the tools were not so good. It was not easy to bore through the stone and the pipes were not so smoothly finished and so nice to look at as they are now. When the pioneers came among us, they brought tools and these the stone workers learned to use with skill. It was not long, however, after the pioneer came that our beds of pipe material were being torn up and put into buildings. In 1880, at Flandreu, which is between Pine Ridge and Rosebud Reservations, someone found the black soapstone. By this time the pipe-makers had files, saws, and other conveniences, so they began making very fine and fancy looking pipes. The bowls were shaped like the buffalo or bear, and one that must have taken a good deal of work was shaped like a locomotive. I had one myself, but gave it away at the time I was made chief.

When tobacco was first burned as a medicine, it was burned full strength, but for smoking it was too strong, so a way was found to make it weaker. The red willow filled this purpose. This willow grows nearly everywhere in this country and turns red in the fall, and for this reason is called the red willow. The Sioux used a great deal of this willow and I have seen them carrying large bundles of it to their tipi to make into smoking weed. The outer bark is peeled off and next to the wood is a soft green bark. This is shaved off and dried in the sun, then mixed with the tobacco.

Of course, before we had fire men did not smoke. But that was a long, long time ago. Only in legends is the story kept of how we found fire and learned how to cook our meat. Our legends say that in that time we ate the meat without cooking, yet it was not exactly raw. It was chipped up fine in thin slices and hung in the sun to dry. At a certain stage it was cured just right.

If left in the sun too long, it would dry more than was necessary to cure and would crumble.

In my day all meat was cooked. There were, however, two parts of the buffalo that we ate raw — the kidney and the liver. Eating a piece of raw liver or kidney now and then is good for the digestion. The Sioux have done this for many years, but I read in a newspaper a few weeks ago that the white doctors are just finding this out. The article that I read claimed that the doctors had found vitamins in raw meat that were nourishing to people who were not getting enough strength out of their food. It seems strange that white people eat so much and some of them get so fat, yet they are not strong, but are ailing and sickly and always going to a doctor. In our natural life we ate a simple diet and did not eat much, yet we were strong and were ashamed of ourselves if we were fat and had no strength.

Some tribes of Indians have made pottery vessels in which to carry water and food, but my people did not. And we did not have tin buckets until the white man came. In place of either of these we used the paunch of the buffalo. The paunch was cleaned and at the top a rawhide rope was drawn through holes by which the top could be closed. If it was to be left open like a bucket, four sticks were thrust through the holes at the top. This utensil usually hung on a pole near the door of the tipi, though in the summer-time it was put up outside under a shade made of limbs of trees. As long as water was kept in this paunch, it stayed soft and rubbery and was easy to handle, but if the water was drawn out for any length of time, it became hard and cracked. If fresh water was put in often, this bucket would last a long time. Furthermore, the water would stay pure and wholesome in this vessel; oftentimes we put leaves of peppermint in to float on top, for we liked both the flavor and odor of the peppermint.

It was a habit with us to drink a great deal of water. We did not have the numerous drinks that the white people have, such as coffee, tea, beer, soda-pop, and cocoa. But after all we had lots of good health. Nowadays there are specialists of all sorts to keep one well. There is the eye specialist and the foot specialist. The dentist looks after the teeth, and another fellow tries to keep you from getting bald-headed. I do not remember ever seeing a bald-headed Sioux in my youth, but now we are afflicted just like the white man. Most of the men of my boyhood days hoped to die on the battlefield so that they would not grow old and useless, for most Indians died of old age and not of disease. Maybe some day all these wise men will be able to point the way for their people to go in order to have health and happiness. At the present time they seem to be helpless to do this.

We not only used the paunch of the buffalo for water-buckets, but for cooking-kettles as well. Before the white man came, we had no iron pots of any kind, but we boiled our meat and had soup just the same. A frame made of four sticks set firmly in the ground held the paunch suspended in the center. This paunch had been cleaned and the top left open like a kettle. The meat was put into this pot with some water and hot stones thrown in. Slowly the meat began to boil. When the stones had cooled, others were put in and the boiling kept going. Finally the pot began to shrink and cook with the meat. When all was done, we drank the soup, ate the meat, and finished up by eating the pot too.

There was left of the meal only the stones. There were no dishes to wash, so it wasn't such a bad system after all. We had no bread, no pies, and no cakes; but we had plenty of fruits and plants to eat. We lived simply but well; and our food was fresh, not stored away in cans for months and months before we ate it. There is no life in food that is kept in this manner and it is not wholesome. We kept cherries and plums all winter by drying them and storing them away in clean rawhide bags. The wild turnip kept all winter, and even after the snow came, the women dug up the wild carrot. So during the long winter we had plenty of meat, fruit, and vegetables. It seemed that everywhere we went there was food waiting for us. In those days the Indian led a happy life.

CHAPTER VI

TANNING, PAINTING, AND DESIGNING

BEFORE we obtained cloth from the white trader, all of our clothing, from headwear to footwear, was made from the tanned skins of animals. The white man also makes many articles of his wearing apparel from the skins of animals, but having other materials from which to cut and sew garments, he does not use skin to the extent that the Indian did. We depended entirely upon the hides of animals to provide us with dresses, skirts, leggins, moccasins, and scarfs or hoods. These garments we wore more or less during all the sea-

sons, except the scarfs or hoods, which we wore
only now and then. Even in coldest weather we
seldom covered our heads.

The simplest way of using the hides was to dry
them, leaving the hair on or taking it off just as
preferred. No process was used, the raw skins
being merely dried by the heat of the sun in summer and by a fire heat in winter. The skin when
dry was hard, stiff, and durable. This raw hide
was used for so many purposes that had the
Indian for some reason been forced to give up the
use of rawhide, he would have found nothing to
take its place. Out of rawhide was made the soles
of moccasins. It was cut into strips and thongs
with which to tie or lace together our travois.
The stirrups and cinches of our saddles were
made from it. Ropes both braided and single
were cut from rawhide. They were easy to
handle and when wet could be knotted so that
when dry would stand any pull. Large boxes like
trunks, lid and all, were made of rawhide and in
them articles of clothing and keepsakes were
kept. These trunks or chests kept their shape as
long as they lasted. Long cylinder-shaped bags

hung in the tipi and held the beautiful feather head-dress which the men wore on dress occasions. These head-dress cases were trimmed down the side with fringes of dyed buckskin. Dyed porcupine quills were also strung on strips of rawhide and used for decorative purposes on bags and boxes. Bags for food were made of rawhide and sometimes were painted in design or otherwise decorated. Handbags or envelope-shaped purses were carried by the women. In them they carried their personal articles of adornment just as women do today. They were carried when visiting or calling and held the awl, or needle, and the sinew or thread, with which the Indian woman worked and found so useful.

Our moccasins were continually wearing out and the women were always making new ones. We wore moccasins the year round, so we needed many pairs, and if the family was large the women of the household were kept busy. Mothers taught their older daughters how to make moccasins and they helped to make them for the younger sisters and brothers. There was only one time when the men made moccasins and that was when the pony or horse needed them to protect his feet. The thick sticky mud of our country sometimes dried on the feet of our horses, making them lame. If neglected, the animal would become sorefooted and unable to travel. So a boot of green hide was wrapped over each foot and tied with rawhide. When dry it was the shape of the horse's hoof and was in no way uncomfortable. This boot kept the foot free from mud and allowed the sore foot to heal, and usually by the time the shoe was worn out the sore foot would be well.

Usually if a hunter went out for a lengthy stay from the village, he would carry with him an extra pair of moccasins. However, if he happened to be away from home and found himself running out of moccasins, he could soon make himself another pair much in the same way as he made them for his pony. He would shoot a buffalo and, skinning the fore leg of the animal from the hoof to the knee, would turn it inside out. He would cut small holes in the hoof end of this strip and lace it up with thongs cut from the hide. This would make for his feet a boot-like covering which he tied about his knees. The skin would be fresh on the outside, but would dry in the weather. And while drying would become well shaped to his feet. It would be hard to find a more resourceful man than the Indian. There is always a way for him to get along, no matter if far out on the plains or in the woods. If he has a bow and arrow, he will get along.

The thick hides of the buffalo, with their soft heavy coat of wool, made the mattress for our bed. It was easy to sleep upon, and in the bitterest weather we kept warm, for our blankets were of buffalo hides also, which were soft and white on one side and of the wool on the other side. Great rugs of these hides covered the floor of the tipi, giving it a look of comfort and keeping it warm in the winter. The most durable of war shields were made from buffalo skin dried with a slow fire heat. So thick and tough was it that the flint and stone arrow points glanced off as if striking an iron surface. Drums, rattles, and breast-pieces were made of the rawhide. The most novel use of rawhide, perhaps, was its use in the sun dance. An uncut, untanned dried skin was the official drum for the sun dance group. The tom-tom was used by the different lodges as they came in and sang ceremonial songs for the dancers, but by the inner group of dancers no tom-tom was permitted. Time was beat for the singing on the dried hide of the buffalo which was thrown on the ground.

The thickest and toughest part of a buffalo hide is on the head, and when removed is deep and round like a bowl. If taken carefully from the head, it has no holes in it and when dry makes an excellent and durable bowl in which to put fruits or meat. In fact, it is used for many purposes in the performance of household duties. Very large bowls or tubs were made by shaping an entire green hide on a mound of earth and staking the edges down. If left on the mound until thoroughly dry, it will form into a deep round bowl large enough for a bathtub.

Much as these raw skins were used, the cured and tanned skins were used as extensively. Both time and skill are required and the coloring and waterproofing of skins becomes an art and science. Most of our garments were made from tanned hide, especially buckskin, yet many articles of utility were made from it too   Since the Sioux have worn skin garments as far back as we know our history, tanning must be a very old practice with them. Again the women do all the tanning, cutting, and sewing of garments, so it must be to them that we are indebted for the art of tanning.

In curing, the hair was left on or taken off just as the wearer wished; also the hides were left their natural white or smoked. There are many shades of brown, and the longer the smoking continued, the darker the skin became.

The skin to be tanned was spread on the ground the hair side next to the earth and the green side up, for it was the side to be worked upon. All meat and membrane was thoroughly scraped off with a sharp bone or flint implement. A mixture of cooked liver and brains was spread on the raw side and the hide folded up and laid away to let the mixture soak into the skin. I am speaking of the large skins, for the tanning of small skins was done without the use of brain and liver mixture. The fresh skins were simply rubbed with the hands until dry.

In four or five days the folded skin was unfolded. By this time it had absorbed enough of
the oils from the brains and liver to make it soft
and easy to handle. One might think that when
the skin was unfolded, it would have a disagree-
able odor, but such was not the case. Nevertheless, it was thoroughly washed with water in
order to remove any particles that might not
have been taken up.

The hide must now be dried, so a stout frame of
poles was built and upon it the skin was tightly
stretched. Holes were cut in the edge of the skin
and it was laced to the poles with long pieces of
rawhide rope. While drying, the skin was rubbed
over with a sandy surfaced stone which acted like
sandpaper, bringing up a soft nap.

When this process was over, the skin was taken
down from the frame. A strong and rough sinew
cord was tightly stretched from a tree branch to
the ground, being firmly fastened to either a root
of the tree or a stake driven into the ground.
The tanner now rubbed the skin back and forth
across the sinew until it was soft and velvety.
If the skin was very large it would take two per-

sons to pull it back and forth, for the large hides were quite heavy. After this sinew finish, the skin would be perfectly soft and smooth. If after the stone finish any rough spots had been left, they would now be gone. The skin was now ready for use as a robe or blanket. On one side the hide would be white and soft, while on the other would be the rich fine hair of the buffalo or deer.

When these beautiful blankets became worn, they would be cut up and made into numerous small but useful articles, such as gloves, scarfs, or belts. For very cold weather moccasins were made with the hair on the inside. Then oftentimes a hunter's fingers would get so cold that it would be hard to use the bow and arrow, so a double garment was worn. This garment or wrap was made with a cape and gloves attached so that the hunter could instantly throw back his cape and not lose his gloves. A belt around the waist kept the wrap from falling to the ground.

The white tan with hair removed was preferred for most garments, although it was not so serviceable as the smoke tan. The women liked much better to wear white dresses and leggins and most of the clothing for children and babes was of soft white buckskin. Also the skins that were used for pillows and for the lighter weight blankets were white. They were kept white and sanitary with a fine white earth powder. This powder was kept stored in bags and was a part of the household necessities. The garments to be cleaned were either rubbed with the dry powder or spread over with a rather dry paste of powder mixed with water. If the paste was used, the garment was folded up and laid away until the paste was dry. When dry the garment was unfolded and the powder rubbed thoroughly into the surface of the skin. This took a little more time, but the skin was purified and white as when first tanned.

There was a great advantage in wearing the brown tanned garments, for even if they got wet they would remain soft and pliable while the white ones got hard and stiff, going back to rawhide. They then had to be retanned. For this reason the clothing that had to be worn in all weathers was made of the brown tan which was waterproof.

The tipis were white when first put up, but after a while became tanned with the smoke from the fire and turned to brown. This waterproofing kept out the rain and the melting snow in the winter and spring. The women tried to do most of the tanning in the summer when it could be done by sun heat. However, it was sometimes necessary to carry on this work in the winter as well. So the hide, which was stretched on a frame, was set over a trench in which there burned a fire of cottonwood bark. This cottonwood bark gave off a steady heat and never threw off sparks. After the skin was taken from over the fire, it was rubbed with the sandstone, and the braided sinew and the winter tanning was just as good as the summer tanning. Sometimes if a skin was not so large that it had to be stretched on an upright frame, it was put over an oval frame of willows built close to the ground. Inside, sagebrush was piled and kept smoldering. The skin, which was staked to the ground, gradually turned to a soft brown.

Useful as rawhide was and beautiful as the soft tanned skins were, the Indian was not satisfied with his handiwork. He wanted even more beauty. Above all things he loved color. All about him were soft tints and vivid colorings. The sky in early morning was a vivid blue and all day it changed its hues. The earth was green with grass and trees and the birds and flowers furnished still greater variety of color for his admiration. Sometimes the rainbow divided the blue sky with color so gorgeous that he longed to keep them with him, so attempted to put them on rawhide and skin. Even the earth was not all one color. Its surface changed too. The soil in one spot would be almost black, in another as white as snow. The hills were colored red, blue, and yellow, and some of the sands and pebbles were silvery in the sun.

As tanning is an old art with our people, so painting is an old art also. And both of these arts are native. They were never imported, but belong to us. Perhaps before we painted on animal skins, we painted our bodies, for in our old legends we are told that it was a custom to color our bodies with paint. And as with tanning it was the woman who did the painting. Occasionally men did this sort of work, but it was considered woman's work and not man's. It must have been the women of the tribe who first learned the uses to which earth could be put. In mixing paints the first experimenters learned that it was better to bake certain clays. So after the soil had been secured, it was mixed with water and patted into loaves and put under hot ashes to bake slowly. The ashes were allowed to cool, then the earth loaves taken out and pounded into a fine powder, to be again mixed with water for paint. In heating the earth paints, the bark of the cottonwood only was used, just as for tanning only this bark was used. The most common of the mineral or earth colors were red, white, and black. Red clay was quite plentiful and white mineral paint was fairly easy to find. Ashes were sometimes used, for gray and black paint was made from charcoal.

As a face paint red was a popular color with Sioux women, just as it is today liked by most women. There was a time when men, women, and children all painted their faces red, but not merely as beautifiers, but for certain good qualities in the soil itself. Earth mixed with water has a healing value and this knowledge has been with our people for a long time. Plasters of mud were used for soothing wounds and for reducing swellings and inflammation. Then there was a certain red soil with which very young babies were rubbed, for it was good for their tender skins. In some of our important ceremonies, the old and wise men plastered their bodies with colored earth. They did this to show that they recognized the healing and cleansing properties of earth.

But not only earth and clays furnished us with many colors. Plants and weeds that grew along the river-banks or on mountains and hillsides, and even at our tipi door, made beautiful and fast colors. The Indian woman's knowledge of using plants for making paints could not have been learned in a short time, but must have been learned by a great many trials. The principal colors were red, blue, green, and yellow, and she knew just what plants produced these colors. Also she knew what season of the year these plants should be gathered, how long they should be soaked in water in order to get proper strength and shade, and just which part of the plant to use and which to discard. Many articles, such as horsehair, porcupine quills, feathers, and buckskin fringe, were dyed for the sole purpose of ornamentation, but articles of daily use, such as shirts, dresses, and quivers were dyed also.

When the artist was ready to begin her work, she spread her hide upon the ground, not upon an easel or frame as is so often pictured. Her tools were a rule and a brush. The rule was a straight, smooth stick of the cherry wood. The stick was eight hands high and with the bark peeled, so as to make it as smooth as possible. The brush was a bone so old that it was porous like a sponge. The paint-cups were turtle-shells, all set about within easy reach of the worker. With this equipment the artist set to work. If a trunk or bag was to be made, the measurements must be correct, so the first thing done was to measure for exact size. The pattern or design the artist would have in her mind. In fact, most of the designing was done by women, and they seem to have established design patterns of a kind that makes them easy to distinguish from

HER TOOLS WERE A RULE AND A BRUSH

those of other tribes. Many of these pretty and interesting patterns were worked out in the evenings by the light of the camp-fire. The earth was smoothed out and served as paper upon which to draw, and a smooth stick was used as a pencil. I have seen my grandmother draw out ashes from the fire and pat them smooth and upon this surface make her marks with the point of her drawing-stick. If the lines she drew were not satisfactory, she would rub them out and try again. When she had found a pattern that pleased her, she put it away in her mind to be used later on some garment she was making. The Indian designer enjoys the work of her creation and takes pride in creating new and pretty designs.

It was a custom with the Sioux to paint their tribal history upon the tipi. The warriors liked to tell their thrilling adventures in this way, so in the olden days there were many tipis in villages all decorated with interesting scenes and figures. Such stories as a warrior touching the enemy with a lance, rescuing a friend from danger, or bravely battling while wounded, would be on the walls of the tipi for all to admire. Sometimes a ceremonial dance was painted with the dancers in full regalia. Then there were many symbols with a fine significance, such as the pipe of peace, the war shield, and the staff or the lance. Oftentimes the buffalo, deer, and eagle were used as subjects, but seldom did the men paint geometric designs as did the women, animals and objects of nature being more to their liking.

The newest of the arts of the Sioux is bead-designing. The white man brought the first colored glass beads the Indian ever saw. The women at once, without being told or having instruction from any one, set about to make use of them. So well have they done that the Sioux are famous for their fine beadwork. So expert did some of these women become that the best of them could sit chatting and work out the most intricate design without counting the number of beads to a stitch. A sense of touch and pattern must be highly developed in order to do this.

I well remember the first beads that our band ever saw and the great curiosity they aroused in us. Every one thought them very beautiful, but, not having seen them before, did not know exactly what to do with them. A train had been wrecked not so far from where we lived and my mother had picked up the beads from the wreckage. She brought them to camp and there was much discussion about them, especially among the women, who immediately began to wonder what they could do with these pretty glass ornaments. After much thought my mother decided they should be put in some way on my blanket. I was her son and only child, and I suppose it was natural that she should think of me first. My blanket was a tanned buffalo hide. On one side the hair had been left, while the other side was a soft white tan. On the white side were the paintings of some historical events which had happened to my father and grandfather. But with all this trimming, mother decided that it should be further decorated with the beads of the white man. So she made a strip of the beads in a design she had worked out herself. When the strip was finished, she sewed it with sinew across the middle of my blanket. Thus I was the first boy on the reservation to wear a beaded blanket, and mother set a fashion which the Sioux like to this day. I have had many blankets, some of them very valuable, but could I now have that blanket, it would be priceless to me. Today the cloth blanket with a beaded band across it is quite commonly worn. Later the beadwork was used to trim handbags, tobacco-pouches, head-bands, feather and quill ends. So much did the Sioux women like these pretty beads and so great was their desire to decorate that I have seen horse blankets and whole sets of harness solidly and gorgeously beaded.

There was a form of designing that was popular only with the young men of the Sioux tribe and that was ice designing. With a sharp bone the artist would cut figures, some of them very difficult, in the ice. If he wanted them to stand out plainly, he would go over the whole picture with dusty or muddy moccasins. These designs were not at all easy to cut, but some of them were very fine and showed great skill.

CHAPTER VII

GAMES

THE Sioux boy had many games that helped to pass the time away. These games were mostly of the sort that tended to develop the muscles and skill of the body, such as throwing, running, jumping, and swimming.

In one village there would be many boys, perhaps forty or fifty, and sometimes more, if it was a large village; so there would always be plenty to join in a game. Everyone got along peacefully and only once in a great while would there be any differences or quarrels among us.

Since our bows and arrows were with us at all times, naturally we had many bow-and-arrow games. In one of these games the leader shot an arrow from his bow, letting it fall where it would. Those who were in the game shot their arrows with the idea of coming as close as possible to the arrow shot by the leader. This game taught us to measure distance, for the boy who came the closest was the winner.

In our shooting games we played with the purpose of becoming good marksmen, and we really took our play seriously, although it was lots of fun too. Shooting at objects that had been thrown in the air was a sport that we all liked. It was great enjoyment, and each one tried to shoot better than the other fellow, yet all the while we were having this fun we realized that, when the actual time came to use our bows and arrows, we must be used to shooting at objects that were moving and not those that were motionless. Animals that we should later hunt would be moving and sometimes swiftly.

A game that developed eye marksmanship was played with rings. We gathered the long slough grass and wound it into bundles with the peel of the willow. The bundle was bent into ring shape and the ends tied together with buckskin strings.

Placing the ring on the end of our arrow, we tossed it as high in the air as we could. Quickly we grasped our bow, placed our arrow, and shot through the ring before it reached the ground.

In late evenings, when we boys had gathered close to the tipis and there was less room for running and throwing games, we often played a quiet game, yet one that required much dexterity. A small pile of brush was built up and the starter of the game would deftly flip his arrow into this pile of brush. This was done by holding the bow as a 'cellist holds his instrument, then using the taut string of the bow as a spring. The arrow must land upright. Each player flipped his arrow just as the leader had and tried to hit the feathers of the upright arrow.

Another throwing game was one which was not thrown with the arm, but from the foot slightly raised. We peeled long, straight, and green willow sticks or other wood that was white under the bark. Then we wrapped the long strips of peeling around our stick, making fancy patterns. We would run the peeling around the stick from end to end like the stripes on stick candy or would lace it on in diamond shape. When we had finished wrapping the stick, it was held over a smoke until the wood was nicely colored where exposed. Then the wrappings of peelings were taken off and the stick was prettily decorated. We held the stick in our right hand, letting it rest lengthwise over the instep of the right foot. As we threw the stick, we raised the foot. With practice this stick could be thrown a long way. The boy who sent his stick the farthest won the game and collected all the sticks of the other boys, and some of them were very pretty with their smoked designs. Arrow-throwing was a great game also, and some of the boys practiced this so much that they could throw an arrow for long distances. I once knew a good thrower who could send his arrow for one hundred yards or more.

A game that could get very exciting for a bunch of little fellows was called 'Wounded Buffalo.' The biggest boy or the one who could run the fastest would be the buffalo. He would carry in his hand a long stick on the end of which was fastened a large piece of cactus with all the thorns left on. There were various kinds of cactus, but we used the round flat-leaved kind that had lots of stickers on both sides and was very uncomfortable to the touch. The piece on the end of the stick would be perhaps the size of a dinner-plate. In the center of this flat surface would be painted a red spot, and this would signify the wounded buffalo. Now the wounded buffalo is some fighter and no easy thing for a man to face. So this big boy was supposed to act in every way like a wounded animal. The rest of us little fellows were, of course, the hunters. You can picture us with naked bodies, hair hanging down our backs, and wearing only moccasins and breechcloths. The likelihood of getting touched with this thorny cactus on the bare body would make any game exciting. In the center was our wounded buffalo charging about, while the rest of us circled him, each with our bow and arrow all set for a shot. The boy who put his arrow through the red spot on the cactus must prepare to run, for immediately the buffalo would charge him.

I remember one funny incident during the excitement of one of these games that still makes me laugh. One day we were playing this game when one of the boys hit the red spot on the cactus, so the chase began. The boy who had hit the wounded buffalo was running with all his strength, but could not help looking back every minute or so to see how close that cactus was getting. It was a matter of outrunning the buffalo or feeling that thorny sting on some part of the bare anatomy. We were all running, too, for the excitement was increasing. None of us observed a high bank right ahead of us and in our path. Not until our escaping warrior had plunged over the bank and out of sight did we realize its presence. The rest of us stopped just in time to avoid going over ourselves. When we looked down, our warrior lay in the dust at the foot of the bank, and the wounded buffalo could only stand and wave the cactus at him, while the rest of us laughed with joy at the situation.

We had ball games of several kinds, and in some of these the whole camp joined. One was a kicking game similar to football. The ball was made of white buckskin filled with buffalo wool.

NONE OF US OBSERVED A HIGH BANK RIGHT AHEAD
OF US

We usually played on moonlight nights, and it was a lively game when men, women, and children took part. Sides were chosen and each side had a tipi. Each group would try to hit the tipi of the other side. There was much running, laughing, and kicking when two or three hundred people were playing.

Another game was played in which only the strong men and boys took part, for it required distance running and much space. The players carried sticks with which to hit the ball and the game was a good deal like hockey. Many times the players ran far out from camp, but of course always came back to the goal which was a tipi and which must be hit with a ball.

A spectacular game was one played at night, and the darker the night the better the game looked. The boys divided evenly in numbers and lined up opposite each other, about sixty or seventy yards apart. Each side made for itself a great number of small balls from the sticky soil or clay which is common where the Sioux lived. On each ball there was stuck a coal of fire. When each side was ready, they threw their balls at one another and the players must step quickly in order to dodge the coals that were flying toward them in great numbers. It was quite a pretty sight at night to see these glowing missiles flying through the air like skyrockets.

There was nothing we boys liked better than running. We loved to run over the ground as fast as we could go, jumping over logs and stones as we went. Our limbs seemed never to tire. What was the use of walking when it was so easy to run? Then there were so many interesting places for a boy to go. It was fun to run far out on the plain through gardens of sunflowers, and just as much to run up a hill to look back to the place from where we had started, or to follow up a stream to watch for swimming-pools and beaver dams. Now and then, however, we got together for a real game to see who could win at foot-racing. Prizes were never given nor was there ever any betting among us. Our pleasure was in the game and in the winning. The best boy won and we were glad to see him do it. Occasionally we raced our ponies in a game, but neither foot-racing nor pony-racing was strictly a boy's game. When the men of two or three villages got together for a day or so, there was usually both foot-racing and horse-racing. Then it was that races were run for stakes. Bows, arrows, quivers, and other personal articles were won and lost, and as a consequence there was much excitement.

In the summer, when we boys were in the water a good deal, we held contests to see who could swim the fastest and who could stay under the water the longest. We were fond of the water, and if we had as a support a root of the cottonwood, which is porous and light, we would swim even a wide river. We also swam across with our ponies. Summer was a most enjoyable season, but still when winter came it did not interfere with our fun. The winters were long and extremely cold. As far as we could see, the world seemed covered with snow and the rivers were frozen hard. But we played just the same. We were strong and enjoyed all seasons equally well.

Many times when our ponies were running, we had seen them slide across a river or stream, never losing a foothold on the slippery surface. So we would run for a stream and try to slide clear across it without falling. We did not have skates, but the rawhide soles of our moccasins after a few trials would get very slippery. We got so we could do some very good balancing, and skated standing up or squatting.

When a crust froze on the snow, we did lots of sledding. Our sleds were made from the ribs of the buffalo. Six or seven of the large ribs, which are curved like the staves of a boat, were lashed together. The ends of the ribs were held the right distance apart with a split cherry stick and laced together with strong strips of rawhide. In this there must be much skill, and when a nice job of lacing was done a fine sled was the result. The ribs of the sled soon became smooth and white as ivory and all that a boy could wish for. To complete the sled a seat was put in the center of it made from the thick wool of the buffalo's head. As now not every boy was fortunate enough to have the finest of sleds. Some of them had to be content with just one rib; but even that was fun, for it would be hard to sit on just one rib and keep it on its course down a steep hill. Then there was the boy who did not have a sled of any kind. So he had to find a way to slide if he was to join in the fun. Wrapping his buffalo robe close about him, he squatted down and fastened it tight about his knees. Then, holding his knees in his arms, down the hill he coasted as fast as the other boys.

The Sioux boys never play marbles, but the girls do. Some marbles were found already shaped smooth and round, but they were not numerous, so the marbles had to be made. And here is where the fathers came in. They would find stones that were nearly round, then would shape and polish them for their daughters. The red sandstone from which the pipe of peace is made was often used and it made pretty marbles, so with all the assortment of material from which these toys were made there was also an assortment of colors. This game was played on the ice. The girls chose sides, an even number to the side. The two groups then sat about fifty feet apart and placed between them in the center of the distance a block of wood about two by two by four inches in size. One side started the game by shooting all the marbles at the block and trying to dislodge it. If they succeeded, they had another chance; if not, the marbles went to the other side. Of course the game ran by rules, so that the most skillful side won. This game was a prize game, the girls playing for a bracelet, hair ornament, or something that was attractive to girls. The winning side took the prize whatever it might be.

Another very nice game that the girls played was called 'Pa-slo-han-pi,' which means to slide. The girls carried long slender and highly polished sticks made of ash as a rule. These wands were taller than the girls and each stick was tipped with the polished horn of the elk or buffalo. A finished stick represented much work and was quite pretty, so was prized by the girls. The stick had been made by a father or grandfather and he had put in many a patient hour polishing and whittling. The Indian way of polishing was to hold the wand in one hand and the knife in the other. As the wand was slowly turned, the knife lightly shaved off the outside of the wood with small short strokes carried always toward the worker. This took a long time and was very tedious work, but when the whittling was done, the wand looked as if it had been rubbed with sandpaper. So that was the way the wands looked that each girl played Pa-slo-han-pi with. The game was to throw these sticks on the ice to see who could throw the farthest. On the ice these sticks would go surprising distances. It was, by the way, considered a very genteel game, and we boys liked to look at the girls out on the ice all dressed up in white buckskins.

We boys did not play the girl's ice game, but we had one of our own called 'Hu-ta-na-cu-te,' and it was a throwing game also. The rib of the buffalo was polished and decorated with eagle feathers which were attached in such a way as to act as a rudder as the rib went through the air. The player threw the Hu-ta-na-cu-te on the ice in such a manner as to make it rise and sail in the air. It sounds very easy to speak of throwing one of these implements, but it in fact took a great deal of practice to play properly. It is said to be a very old game of the Sioux.

So either in summer or winter we had interesting times.

CHAPTER VIII

HOW CHIEFS ARE MADE

ONE day in our village there was unusual excitement. Other bands of Sioux kept coming in and putting up their tipis and soon our village was three or four times larger than it had been. The circle was so large that the tipi farthest away looked very small in the distance. Indians were crossing back and forth visiting friends, for when several bands got together it was a great time to look up old friends and to get news concerning the whereabouts and doings of other bands. By way of entertainment small groups of Indians, all dressed up, were marching from tipi to tipi singing for those inside. Everyone seemed to be having a good time. We little fellows were enjoying ourselves also, meeting and getting acquainted with other boys whom we had not known before. These little fellows had come riding their ponies and we had looked them over showing ours to them at the same time.

Preparations were being made for a great celebration. Here and there a tipi stood out a little in front of the line of tipis and these belonged to the chiefs. I could see that many chiefs had arrived. In the center of this great circle of tipis an arbor of limbs and boughs had been built that would shelter many people.

That night the fires that burned in the village seemed numberless to me. I went to bed bewildered, excited, and happy, for I had had a wonderful day among so many new acquaintances.

The next day all the people gathered in the arbor or hall to listen to the council of chiefs. In the center of this enclosure the chiefs and headmen sat in a semicircle, a fire burning in front of them. The people filled all the rest of the space. One chief after another arose and talked, while the others listened respectfully. Many things were talked about that were for the good of the tribe. And many things were discussed and settled.

Then one of the chiefs stood up and told the people that a new chief was to be chosen. This was a very serious matter and not to be done in haste, but with care and much council. No man must be chosen unless he had shown himself fully worthy of the honor and no man would be chosen unless he had the respect and confidence of all the people. Even though a young man was the son or grandson of a chief, he would not be chosen for this high office if he had displeased his people. The young man chosen had proved himself good and brave. And now the chiefs had decided upon the right man. There was at once great curiosity. Among the crowd there were fathers and mothers who had raised their sons to be true and brave. They were proud of these sons and were hoping that the honor would fall to them. Many young men had striven to be upright and trustworthy and were anxious to be chosen. But all were filled with curiosity.

Two chiefs withdrew from the others for a moment's conversation. They then walked directly to a young man named Hollow Horn Bear. Without saying a word, they each took Hollow Horn Bear by an arm and marched him between them to the center of the council. A chief who held the pipe of peace walked to the fire and lighted it. He approached the young man and with great dignity lifted the pipe to the heavens, then east, south, west, north, and lastly to the earth. When finished with this silent ceremony, he offered the pipe to the young man, who puffed it twice. This meant that the pipe was accepted and with it the responsibility of chief of his tribe. Hollow Horn Bear thus acknowledged his gratefulness for the honor bestowed upon him by his people and his readiness to make the sacrifices to prove it.

Hollow Horn Bear knew that to be leader and adviser of his people he must be honest and reliable, and that his word once given in promise must never be taken back. He knew that he must be a man of will power, standing for the right no matter what happened to him personally; that he must have strength of purpose, allowing no influence to turn him from doing what was best for the tribe. He must be willing to serve his people without thought of pay. He must be utterly unselfish and kind-hearted to the old and poor and stand ever ready to give to those in need. Above all, he must be unafraid to deal equal justice to all.

Now all these virtues mean one thing, and that is bravery. A Sioux boy was taught to be brave always. It was not sufficient to be brave enough to go to war. He must be brave enough to make personal sacrifices and to think little of personal gain. To be brave was the supreme test of a Sioux boy, and this bravery might receive a greater test in times of peace than in times of war.

The pipe of peace was the strongest symbol in all the world for the Sioux Indian, so that is why Hollow Horn Bear was offered the pipe upon which to take his oath of chieftainship. This satisfied the people also, for they knew that once he had sworn by the pipe he would never go back on his word. There is a saying, 'An Indian never goes back on his word'; and that was true in the olden days. The strength of the pipe was such that a Sioux sworn by it never failed even in the face of death. Another thing, to be entitled to carry the pipe in one of the beautiful painted or decorated bags which the Sioux make showed that the one so entitled held the highest position in the tribe.

When the pipe ceremony for Hollow Horn Bear had been completed, a second chief came and stood in front of him. This second chief talked straight to Hollow Horn Bear, but in a voice that all could hear. He reminded the newly made chief that he had received good training from a good father. Iron Shield, who was Hollow Horn Bear's father, had passed on, but still the people remembered him as a good man and all were grateful to him for raising a son who was worthy to be chief. When this chief had finished talking, it was plain to see that Hollow Horn Bear was very proud to hear his father praised.

A third chief now stood in front of Hollow Horn Bear and spoke. The speech of the second chief had been long and full of praise, but the speech of the third chief was short. He said, 'Hollow Horn Bear, you have heard your father praised for the things he did for his people. The trust that we had for him we now put in you. There is much that you, too, can do for your people.' That was all. That evening all the Indians gathered in full regalia and there was much singing and dancing.

The next day festivities continued. It was the day for the newly made chief to begin to serve his people and he did so by showing how great his generosity was.

Again all the people were assembled in the council hall in the center of the village. Hollow Horn Bear came bringing to them all of his possessions. His friends were helping him carry them to the center of the circle. These things were to be distributed as gifts among the poor and needy. There were bows and arrows in painted quivers, head-dresses, saddles, bridles, beautifully painted robes, and other articles prized by the Sioux. Songs of praise were sung for Chief Hollow Horn Bear and for every song a gift was given to someone who was in need. At last everything was gone and Hollow Horn Bear went home a poor man, but with a satisfaction that made him happy. The exchange in goods that he had made for the trust of his people made him proud and more determined than ever to be brave.

Generosity is a mark of bravery, so all Sioux boys were taught to be generous. If a Sioux boy sees an old man or woman passing, he often runs out and asks them into the tipi. The boy's mother is always glad to see her boy so thoughtful and offers the old man or woman something to eat. The old people feel very grateful for this attention and give thanks in either words or songs of praise.

I can well remember when we first learned to make and drink coffee. It tasted bitter, and we thought it good for medicine, so we called it 'black medicine.' The old people especially grew fond of it, so it was a great treat to them to be called into a tipi some early cool morning by some thoughtful young person and given a nice hot drink. At first we boys did not care much about drinking 'medicine,' but after a while we got to liking it also. As we played about the village, we would smell the coffee boiling and would begin a search for the tipi where it was being made. We did not wait to be asked in, for it was not impolite to let anyone know that we liked coffee and wished to have some. So we quietly walked in and seated ourselves, and when the woman began serving, she would not overlook us. Whenever we had finished drinking and eating whatever eatable had been handed us, we simply handed back the cup from which we had been drinking and said, 'Aunt, here is your dish.' This was enough to say in order to be polite and gracious. We did not make long speeches. When an Indian is visiting a friend and it is time to go, he simply arises and says, 'I must now go.'

The Sioux boy not only earns any honor which he may receive, but he also earns his name by which he will be known when he becomes a man. His name at birth is selected by his parents or by some of his relations, and this he keeps until he is old enough to earn one for himself. A Sioux boy was supposed to distinguish himself in some way or prove his bravery or worth. He would then be privileged to take a name indicating what this worthy act was. So from childhood up he longed for a chance to do some brave deed. If in battle he would try to save a friend who was in greater danger than himself. If he chanced to be severely wounded, he would go on fighting as long as possible, for he wanted to endure hardship without complaint. Perhaps he would accept a dangerous mission as a scout into the camp of the enemy or maybe he would take the test of 'touching the enemy.' If he could do this and get away unharmed, he would then become known as a very brave man.

'Touching the enemy,' as the Sioux called it, was done in this way: A young warrior on meeting an armed member of the enemy tribe would throw his own weapons away, keeping for his protection only his shield. In his hand he would carry a long staff decorated with eagle feathers which was a sort of flag or banner for the Sioux. With only the shield over his breast and the lance in his hand, he would ride close to the enemy. When close enough to touch the enemy with the point of the staff or lance, as it is usually called, he would lightly strike the enemy's body with the tip of the lance, then ride back out of danger as fast as possible. As he turned from his enemy, he would throw his shield from his breast to his back to avoid if possible the arrows aimed at him. Many times a warrior was fortunate enough to get away unharmed, but, on the other hand, oftentimes in performing this feat he would be badly wounded. In either case he would be honored among his people for having been brave enough to ride unarmed up to an enemy waiting to shoot him. When he returned home, a big feast and dance was held for him. His mother and sisters would sing his praise and the whole tribe would do him honor. At this ceremony he would receive a new name by which he would thereafter be known.

While my father was young he was called Spotted Horse. His father, who was One Horse, had at one time captured a number of spotted horses from an enemy tribe, so earned the right to call his son by that name. So my father used the name Spotted Horse until old enough to go on the warpath and earn a name for himself. This he did at the age of eighteen. His party had met and routed the Pawnees. All had fled except

THE PAWNEE SHOT HIS ARROW

one who for some reason had been left behind. Though this brave Pawnee was well armed and an expert with bow and arrow, father thought it a good time to 'touch the enemy.' Throwing his weapons away and holding a decorated lance of wood in his hand, he started riding for the Pawnee. The Pawnee stood with drawn bow. When close enough, father touched the man with the tip of his wooden lance, then rode as quickly as possible back to his comrades. The Pawnee shot his arrow, striking my father in the arm and making a severe wound. Father continued the fight without stopping to have his wound attended to, and thus earned the name of Standing Bear. The bear is a brave animal and often stands and fights, though wounded, so my father, being brave as a wounded bear and fighting while his blood was flowing, was called Standing Bear. When I was born, my father had earned the right to call me Plenty Kill, for he had killed many of the enemy.

All of my brothers had names that signified something to the family. One was named Sorrel Horse. Father once had a sorrel horse shot from under him. By naming my brother this, the deed was kept in the memory of the family and tribe. Another brother was named Never Defeated. Father had never been defeated at anything he had undertaken, so this name, too, carries with it a memory. In the names of his sons the history of his own life was kept fresh and living even after he had passed away.

The girls, not earning their names as did the boys, were given names that had a meaning for the family and these names they kept throughout life. One of my sisters was named Feather Weaver, for my father had many feather decorations. Another sister was named Two Staffs, for father belonged to two lodges and each had given him a feather-decorated staff. Another sister was named Yellow Bird by an aunt, and this name, of course, meant something to that aunt.

When I had grown old enough to go on the warpath, there were no more wars for the Indian, so I did not have a chance to earn my name as did my father. I can remember when I was only a little boy wishing that I could prove to my father that I was brave too. I had my chance when eleven years old. By that time the Sioux had laid down their weapons and were living a peaceful life. One day some white people came among us and called a meeting of the parents. We children did not know what it was all about, but I sensed something serious, for my father was very thoughtful for a time. Then he asked me one day if I would like to go away with the white people. They had come after some boys and girls and wanted to take them a long way off to a place about which we knew nothing. I consented at once, though I could think of nothing else but that these white people wanted to take us far away and kill us. I had never heard of a school, and what else could these white people want with a little long-haired Indian boy who wore nothing but a breech-cloth and moccasins? To me it meant death, but bravery was part of my blood, so I did not hesitate. Years after, when I had returned to my people to help them in every way I could to acquire the white man's way, they met in council and called me Chief Standing Bear.

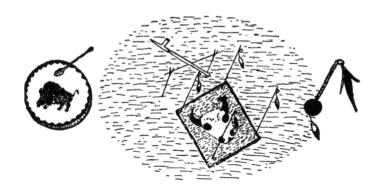

CHAPTER IX

MEDICINE MEN AND MUSIC

AMONG the most important men in any Sioux village were the medicine men. We had great faith in them and respected them for their powers to cure us. They became very wise. They helped the ailing, cured the sick, and did many other things that were wonderful but mysterious to us, yet they never went to school and they had no books to study from. Instead, they went into the mountains alone and unarmed. There they stayed for days fasting and praying. They asked the Great Spirit for the knowledge and power that would enable them to go back to their people and cure the sick and wounded and make them well. These men were earnest and devout. They sincerely desired to be of some use to their tribe and to help those in need.

No man in all the tribe was more admired for his power and knowledge than the medicine man, and all boys grew up hoping some day to be one. We knew that in some way he got his power from Nature, so we searched Nature for this power too. In a measure we sensed the energy and power in every common thing about us, and so we looked at the trees, the cliffs, the streams, the stones, the birds, and everything else, and wished for power. And as we did so we felt the power within us grow.

But not every one succeeded in becoming a medicine man. Only a few became wise enough and strong enough. Even men who became chiefs were unable to become medicine men.

When a young man has decided to make the final test, he immediately purifies himself with the sweat bath. A trusted friend selects for him a distant and secluded spot where he can fast without interruption. For after the fast has begun, nothing must happen to disturb his quiet communion with Nature. The spot of prayer and fasting is marked with four poles eight or ten feet high set at the four corners. The young man takes with him the sacred pipe and his buffalo robe. He goes with a receptive mind and soul ready to see all and hear all. After days of fasting and praying, the young man feels himself getting closer in touch with mysterious powers. Each day he becomes weaker and weaker and soon he loses consciousness and goes into a deep sleep. It is in this sleep that the Great Mystery comes to him in the form of some bird or animal and talks with him. They have come to impart to him a secret of value and to share with him some of their power. Sometimes they bring a fetish of some kind or an herb or root that has great healing power, or it may be a song to sing at the bedside of the sick. But whatever is brought is useful and powerful. The sleeping man's mind is most vivid. He remembers everything with exact clearness. Even though he has never seen the herb or plant, when he awakens he will know it when he sees it, and where to find it.

It is difficult to learn a song once sung, but the song the sleeping man hears he will forever after remember.

After the fast is over and the man has had his vision, he returns to his village and is henceforth called a 'dreamer.' If the bear has come to him he will be a 'bear dreamer'; if the duck has come to him he will be a 'duck dreamer'; and so on, always giving credit to the animal or bird who will assist him in his cures.

When we were children and we saw the medicine man go into a tipi where there was illness, we stayed away, for we felt that the Great One was there with this man. The sacredness of the ceremony and our reverence for the man made us very humble.

One day we saw several of our young men returning from a war party. Great excitement was in camp. As they came near, we could see that one of the young men had something the matter with his leg. It was swinging back and forth as he sat on his horse. When he got into the village, he took hold of his leg and swung it across his horse. Then he hopped down and went into the tipi. We all watched him, for he seemed to be so brave. We children knew that soon the medicine man would be there, so ran off to play. We thought no more about him until a few days later, when we saw him hopping around. Rawhide splints were held to his leg with rawhide strips and he carried a cane made from the branch of a tree. We had no crutches in those days, but the crippled and the old people used very tall canes something like a shepherd's crook. We never had any fear of blood poison, for our blood was clean and pure. The young man had every faith in the medicine man and he was well in a surprisingly short time.

The first great cure that I can remember was for a boy who had Saint Vitus's Dance. We knew nothing of this sickness until the white people came, so we called this disease 'skan-skan wasicun,' or, 'shakes like a white man.' We thought it so queer to see this boy shake all over even when he was standing still, so when we heard our people talking about the medicine ceremony for him, we were all anxious to see it.

The parents of this boy had put up a large tipi

away from the rest with the door facing the east. When the medicine man came, we all gathered around in a big circle. Every one was very quiet. The medicine man was painted red and wore only a breech-cloth. In his right hand he carried a rattle and in his left a tom-tom. He went into the tipi with the sick boy and soon came out with the sick boy just in front of him. The boy's body was also painted red and he wore a breech-cloth just like the medicine man. The medicine man walked the boy to the four corners of the earth or the four directions, all the while chanting his medicine song and keeping time with the tom-tom. The last stop was made at the north, and when this journey to the four directions or the four winds, as the Indian calls it, had been made, it formed a square about the tipi. The medicine man then took the boy back into the tipi. A few days later, when we saw this boy, he was all right. Since he did not shake like a white man, we let him play with us.

One thing that the medicine man nearly always used in his ceremonies was music, both singing and playing. For keeping time with his singing he used a tom-tom or rattle. And sometimes he played a whistle.

These instruments were held sacred by the medicine man and one might never see them unless sometime they became sick or were in some way favored. To handle them carelessly or to permit every one to gaze at them would cause them to lose some of their power. The rattles, on which symbols may be painted which only the medicine man understands, are kept in prettily painted rawhide bags. In these bags are also kept the herbs and other things needed in his cures.

When the medicine man comes to the tipi of his patient, all must be quiet, so some member of the family keeps watch outside to see that no one makes a noise.

The first thing the medicine man does is to build a little square altar of earth on the ground near the bed of the sick person. At the four corners there are placed four upright sticks. These sticks are painted in attractive colors and the altar is beautified with a design worked out in colored earth. Then the medicine man sings for the patient, for the Indian sings for all occasions. He believes that singing brings him closer to the higher powers than anything else he can do. He believes that a single voice is strong enough for the Great Spirit to hear.

When the song has been finished, the medicine man takes from his bags the herbs which he either soaks or boils in water. By the time the sick person has been given some of this purifying herb tea, he feels better. Sometimes the medicine man tells to the sick person the story of how he went to the mountains to fast and pray and of the wonderful vision he had while there. The patient often gets so interested that he forgets he is sick and sometimes never needs another treatment.

The rattle of the medicine man is made of rawhide, cut into shape while green and sewed together like the covering of a baseball, except that a strip is left on so that the handle will have a covering of rawhide. The pieces of rawhide are sewed almost together, a little opening being left through which sand is poured so that the hide would dry round and hollow. When dry, the sand was poured out and pebbles put in. Next a stick for a handle was put in. The handle was run clear to the opposite side of the rattle so as to make it very firm. If not put in to extend clear to the other side and press tightly against the rawhide, it would work loose very quickly. This is quite an important thing to remember. As soon as the handle is securely fastened, it is ready to be covered with the strip of rawhide that has been left for that purpose. When the rawhide is thoroughly dry, it is ready for decoration.

In singing and dancing, the rattle gives a sense of rhythm which with the Indian must be very exact. It is a very fine sight to see a large number of dancers performing, all keeping step with perfect time and every rattle moving in the same way at the same time.

The Fox Lodge now uses the tin rattle. When the white traders first came among us, they brought baking powder in tin cans. We thought these cans more useful than the baking powder. So we just emptied out the powder and used the can. The top was put on the can and a wooden handle tightly fastened in, then the whole thing covered with beads. The top of the rattle and the end of the handle were finished with tassels of brightly colored feathers. Of course, before the handle was put in a dozen or so hard pebbles were placed in the can. Some of these rattles were covered with very fine beadwork and decorated with colored hair and porcupine quills on the handle. Also they were something new to the Sioux and for this reason considered more desirable than the rawhide rattles. Only two of these were used in the Fox Lodge, and these were not given to the important members, but to the young men and boys to encourage them to do good things and to be brave. If he could not go on the warpath and do some brave deed, he would give a feast and feed the poor. In the feast dance he was entitled to use the rattle. If he did go on the warpath and returned home a brave warrior, his mother and sister would dance for him and use the rattle to show their pride in him.

I remember one young man who went to war and came home a very brave man. Just what he did I do not recall, but something he did made his family very proud. He had three beautiful sisters and they were much admired by the whole village for their good looks. One of the three sisters wore the brother's head-dress, one took his lance and one took his dance rattle and went from tipi to tipi singing the praises of their brother. It was a great sight, and the whole camp looked on while the sisters did honor to their brother.

The Brave Lodge uses a very peculiar-shaped rattle. It is shaped like a hollow ring or doughnut, but larger. Only two rattles can be used in this lodge and by the two men who are supposed to be the bravest. The rattles are cut and sewed while the rawhide is green. Sand holds it in shape while drying. When dry, the handle is put in and tightly fastened. Then the whole rattle is painted red, this being the color of the Brave Lodge. The men who join the Brave Lodge do so with the idea of trying to be brave and making a great name for themselves.

There was a time when the Sioux had no drums, but he sang before he had this instrument. Before the first tom-tom was made, the singer beat his chest with his fists and this way kept time with his voice. So the Sioux have been singing for a long time and some of their songs are very old. Now there are several kinds of drums made. One way is to make the shell or band of elm wood, which bends very easily and is very light in weight. In the skin of the buffalo there is a thin skin. This is stretched over the frame tightly on one side and on the other side gathered together and held with a rawhide string. This is an excellent drum while it lasts, but the skin from the stomach of the buffalo is not very durable. When once it has cracked, there is, of course, no sound in the drum.

Another way in which the Sioux made tom-toms was to make a case as in the first description, but the skin was not tied on. Small holes were drilled around the frame a little way apart, then a deerskin stretched over it and held in place with wooden pins driven through the skin and fitted into the holes.

Still another way was to take a hollow log and stretch skins over both ends, lacing the skins back and forth over the body of the log. Large drums were usually made in this way. There was what we called the water drum, made from a log also, but not hollowed clear through. A solid bottom was left in one end and the log filled with water. The skin was stretched over the open end. The sound of this drum depended upon keeping the skin wet, so when it began to dry, the drum was tipped over until the skin was again wet.

There is much difference in the sound of drums and a great deal depends on the skill of the maker. Some of the sounds are high and thin and they range to a deep and mellow tone that is very stirring. A good tom-tom player can do very much with the sticks in beating time and rhythm, and one who is used to dancing to this wonderful instrument feels the blood stirring within him at its sound.

Most of the big drums were without decoration, but the small tom-toms were nearly always painted in a most interesting and sometimes meaningful manner. The medicine man often painted on his drum the form of the animal whose power he used to heal the sick. For instance, the Elk Dreamer medicine man may paint the head of an elk on his drum, but since all Nature is related and the medicine man looks to Nature for help, he may have, besides the elk's head, other animal or bird paintings and even insects such as the spider. The Bear Dreamer may put on his drum the feet of the bear, while the Thunder Dreamer may use the zigzag lines of lightning. Whatever the decoration, it would be an acknowledgment of debt to natural powers.

There is a time-keeping instrument which I think must be almost as old as the tom-tom. It was made of wood and the Sioux translation of it is 'wood on wood.' This instrument was made of a straight stick notched on one side and smooth on the other. The player held the instrument in the left hand and with another stick in the right hand played up and down on the notches just as a violin is played. When it was keeping time with the tom-tom, it sounded very good, but we seldom see one any more.

In the Sioux tribe we used the whistle very much and it too must be a very old instrument. In the springtime when the willows are green, a small branch or twig was cut the proper length for a whistle. The peel was loosened by tapping evenly and steadily on another stick or something hard. If done right, the inside stalk would drop right out of the peel, leaving a hollow stick which would be turned into a whistle by making a notch in it at the proper place and putting in a piece of pitch gum near the mouth end.

The best whistles, however, were made of eagle bones taken from the wing of the bird. The bone was notched also and a piece of gum placed where it would make the pleasantest tone. The pine gum was first chewed, then pressed into place with a stick. These eagle-bone whistles were used in nearly all of the ceremonies of the Sioux. Sometimes the medicine man used them and at other times a large number of dancers all had one in their mouths. It was believed that these whistles were useful in battle. A great number of warriors on horseback would supply themselves with whistles. In the attack they would play these whistles and the music was supposed to make the enemy nervous while it made the musicians braver. In the sun dance there was a band of singers and a band of whistlers who performed without stopping for three days. At first their tones were clear and loud, but toward the last, when all were weary, the tones of the whistler would be very faint. Only in the sun dance were these whistles decorated with the eagle feathers or down. More often, though, the mothers and sisters decorated them with the dyed porcupine quills.

\ There is one instrument that is used for just one purpose, and that is the flute. Since on this flute nothing but the love song was played, we called it the 'love flute.' In Sioux it is called the 'la-la' and is a native instrument, for we were using it when the white man came. It requires some skill to make this instrument, for it is in several pieces. The flutes that were made long ago were all of cedar, as it chipped easily with a flint tool. A cedar limb was split into equal halves right down the center lengthwise. These two pieces were then hollowed out and the mouth-piece shaped. Between the mouth-piece and the main air chamber a partition was left in the wood. Over this was placed a thin sliding bone held in place by a saddle cut of wood. The saddle was tied on with a piece of buckskin. Lastly six finger-holes were cut into the flute at the proper places. The several pieces of this flute were put together with glue of which a supply was always on hand. The neck of the buffalo or horns of the elk were cut into small pieces and put to boil in the paunch kettle. As the glue rose to the top it was skimmed off on a stick. The stick was turned around slowly, the glue sticking to it in long clear strings. When enough of the glue had stuck to the end of the stick to make a ball, the other end of the stick was sharpened and stuck into the ground so that the mass would dry in the air. When dry, it looked like glass and was very hard. It was convenient to carry by just dropping a stick into the quiver. Neither cold nor heat affected it and it never melted and ran over the arrows nor stuck to the quiver. When ready to use it, we wet it with our tongues and held it a moment over the fire and we had a liquid glue. Nothing that I have ever seen manufactured is as good as this glue. When two pieces are put together with Indian glue, it is just as good as one piece.

Long before the Indian was skillful enough to make musical instruments, he composed and sang songs in which he put the history of his tribe. He told of his wars, his ceremonies, and his travels. There were brave songs, medicine songs, war songs, songs of reverence to the Great Mystery, and love songs. Then the lodges had their songs which only lodge members sang. Even the individual had songs which he composed for himself alone. These songs were regarded as personal property and one would be committing theft to take the song of another. The composers sometimes gave away their songs, making a present of them just as they might any article of personal possession. But no matter what event in life the Indian faced — he sang.

CHAPTER X

AT LAST I KILL A BUFFALO

At last the day came when my father allowed me to go on a buffalo hunt with him. And what a proud boy I was!

Ever since I could remember my father had been teaching me the things that I should know and preparing me to be a good hunter. I had learned to make bows and to string them; and to make arrows and tip them with feathers. I knew how to ride my pony no matter how fast he would go, and I felt that I was brave and did not fear danger. All these things I had learned for just this day when father would allow me to go with him on a buffalo hunt. It was the event for which every Sioux boy eagerly waited. To ride side by side with the best hunters of the tribe, to hear the terrible noise of the great herds as they ran, and then to help to bring home the kill was the most thrilling day of any Indian boy's life. The only other event which could equal it would be the day I went for the first time on the warpath to meet the enemy and protect my tribe.

On the following early morning we were to start, so the evening was spent in preparation. Although the tipis were full of activity, there was no noise nor confusion outside. Always the evening before a buffalo hunt and when every one was usually in his tipi, an old man went around the circle of tipis calling, 'I-ni-la,' 'I-ni-la,' not loudly, but so every one could hear. The old man was saying, 'Keep quiet,' 'Keep quiet.' We all knew that the scouts had come in and reported buffalo near and that we must all keep the camp in stillness. It was not necessary for the old man to go into each tipi and explain to the men that tomorrow there would be a big hunt, as the buffalo were coming. He did not order the men to prepare their weapons and neither did he order the mothers to keep children from crying. The one word, 'I-ni-la,' was sufficient to bring quiet to the whole camp. That night there would be no calling or shouting from tipi to tipi and no child would cry aloud. Even the horses and dogs obeyed the command for quiet, and all night not a horse neighed and not a dog barked. The very presence of quiet was everywhere. Such is the orderliness of a Sioux camp that men, women, children, and animals seem to have a common understanding and sympathy. It is no mystery but natural that the Indian and his animals understand each other very well both with words and without words. There are words, however, that the Indian uses that are understood by both his horses and dogs. When on a hunt, if one of the warriors speaks the word 'A-a-ah' rather quickly and sharply, every man, horse, and dog will stop instantly and listen. Not a move will be made by an animal until the men move or speak further. As long as the hunters listen, the animals will listen also.

The night preceding a buffalo hunt was always

an exciting night, even though it was quiet in
camp. There would be much talk in the tipis
around the fires. There would be sharpening
of arrows and of knives. New bow-strings
would be made and quivers would be filled with
arrows.

It was in the fall of the year and the evenings
were cool as father and I sat by the fire and talked
over the hunt. I was only eight years of age, and
I know that father did not expect me to get
a buffalo at all, but only to try perhaps for a
small calf should I be able to get close enough to
one. Nevertheless, I was greatly excited as I sat
and watched father working in his easy, firm
way.

I was wearing my buffalo-skin robe, the hair
next to my body. Mother had made me a rawhide belt and this, wrapped around my waist,
held my blanket on when I threw it off my
shoulders. In the early morning I would wear it,
for it would be cold. When it came time to shoot,
I should not want my blanket but the belt would
hold it in place.

You can picture me, I think, as I sat in the

glow of the camp-fire, my little brown body bare to the waist watching, and listening intently to my father. My hair hung down my back and I wore moccasins and breech-cloth of buckskin. To my belt was fastened a rawhide holster for my knife, for when I was eight years of age we had plenty of knives. I was proud to own a knife, and this night I remember I kept it on all night. Neither did I lay aside my bow, but went to sleep with it in my hand, thinking, I suppose, to be all the nearer ready in the morning when the start was made.

Father sharpened my steel points for me and also sharpened my knife. The whetstone was a long stone which was kept in a buckskin bag, and sometimes this stone went all over the camp; every tipi did not have one, so we shared this commodity with one another. I had as I remember about ten arrows, so when father was through sharpening them I put them in my rawhide quiver. I had a rawhide quirt, too, which I would wear fastened to my waist. As father worked, he knew I was watching him closely and listening whenever he spoke. By the time all preparations had been made, he had told me just how I was to act when I started out in the morning with the hunters.

We went to bed, my father hoping that to-morrow would be successful for him so that he could bring home some nice meat for the family and a hide for my mother to tan. I went to bed, but could not go to sleep at once, so filled was I with the wonderment and excitement of it all. The next day was to be a test for me. I was to prove to my father whether he was or was not justified in his pride in me. What would be the result of my training? Would I be brave if I faced danger and would father be proud of me? Though I did not know it that night I was to be tried for the strength of my manhood and my honesty in this hunt. Something happened that day which I remember above all things. It was a test of my real character and I am proud to say that I did not find myself weak, but made a deci-sion that has been all these years a gratification to me.

The next morning the hunters were catching their horses about daybreak. I arose with my father and went out and caught my pony. I wanted to do whatever he did and show him that he did not have to tell me what to do. We brought our animals to the tipi and got our bows and arrows and mounted. From over the village came the hunters. Most of them were leading their running horses. These running horses were anxious for the hunt and came prancing, their ears straight up and their tails waving in the air. We were joined with perhaps a hundred or more riders, some of whom carried bows and arrows and some armed with guns.

The buffalo were reported to be about five or six miles away as we should count distance now. At that time we did not measure distance in miles. One camping distance was about ten miles, and these buffalo were said to be about one half camping distance away.

Some of the horses were to be left at a stopping-place just before the herd was reached. These horses were pack-animals which were taken along to carry extra blankets or weapons. They were trained to remain there until the hunters came for them. Though they were neither hobbled nor tied, they stood still during the shooting and noise of the chase.

My pony was a black one and a good runner. I felt very important as I rode along with the hunters and my father, the chief. I kept as close to him as I could.

Two men had been chosen to scout or to lead the party. These two men were in a sense policemen whose work it was to keep order. They carried large sticks of ash wood, something like a policeman's billy, though longer. They rode ahead of the party while the rest of us kept in a group close together. The leaders went ahead until they sighted the herd of grazing buffalo. Then they stopped and waited for the rest of us to ride up. We all rode slowly toward the herd, which on sight of us had come together, although they had been scattered here and there over the plain. When they saw us, they all ran close together as if at the command of a leader. We continued riding slowly toward the herd until one of the leaders shouted, 'Ho-ka-he!' which means, 'Ready, Go!' At that command every man started for the herd. I had been listening, too, and the minute the hunters started, I started also.

Away I went, my little pony putting all he had into the race. It was not long before I lost sight of father, but I kept going just the same. I threw my blanket back and the chill of the autumn morning struck my body, but I did not mind. On I went. It was wonderful to race over the ground with all these horsemen about me. There was no shouting, no noise of any kind except the pounding of the horses' feet. The herd was now running and had raised a cloud of dust. I felt no fear until we had entered this cloud of dust and I could see nothing about me — only hear the sound of feet. Where was father? Where was I going? On I rode through the cloud, for I knew I must keep going.

Then all at once I realized that I was in the midst of the buffalo, their dark bodies rushing all about me and their great heads moving up and down to the sound of their hoofs beating upon the earth. Then it was that fear overcame me and I leaned close down upon my little pony's body and clutched him tightly. I can never tell you how I felt toward my pony at that moment. All thought of shooting had left my mind. I was seized by blank fear. In a moment or so, however, my senses became clearer, and I could distinguish other sounds beside the clatter of feet. I could hear a shot now and then and I could see the buffalo beginning to break up into small bunches. I could not see father nor any of my companions yet, but my fear was vanishing and I was safe. I let my pony run. The buffalo looked too large for me to tackle, anyway, so I just kept going. The buffalo became more and more scattered. Pretty soon I saw a young calf that looked about my size. I remembered now what father had told me the night before as we sat about the fire. Those instructions were important for me now to follow.

I was still back of the calf, being unable to get alongside of him. I was anxious to get a shot, yet afraid to try, as I was still very nervous. While my pony was making all speed to come alongside, I chanced a shot and to my surprise my arrow landed. My second arrow glanced along the back of the animal and sped on between the horns, making only a slight wound. My third arrow hit a spot that made the running beast slow up in his gait. I shot a fourth arrow, and though it, too, landed it was not a fatal wound. It seemed to me that it was taking a lot of shots, and I was not proud of my marksmanship. I was glad, however, to see the animal going slower and I knew that one more shot would make me a hunter. My horse seemed to know his own importance. His two ears stood straight forward and it was not necessary for me to urge him to get closer to the buffalo. I was soon by the side of the buffalo and one more shot brought the chase to a close. I jumped from my pony, and as I stood by my fallen game, I looked all around wishing that the world could see. But I was alone. In my determination to stay by until I had won my buffalo, I had not noticed that I was far from every one else. No admiring friends were about, and as far as I could see I was on the plain alone. The herd of buffalo had completely disappeared. And as for father, much as I wished for him, he was out of sight and I had no idea where he was.

I stood and looked at the animal on the ground.

ONE MORE SHOT BROUGHT THE CHASE TO A CLOSE

I was happy. Every one must know that I, Ota K'te, had killed a buffalo. But it looked as if no one knew where I was, so no one was coming my way. I must then take something from this animal to show that I had killed it. I took all the arrows one by one from the body. As I took them out, it occurred to me that I had used five arrows. If I had been a skillful hunter, one arrow would have been sufficient, but I had used five. Here it was that temptation came to me. Why could I not take out two of the arrows and throw them away? No one would know, and then I should be more greatly admired and praised as a hunter. As it was, I knew that I should be praised by father and mother, but I wanted more. And so I was tempted to lie.

I was planning this as I took out my skinning knife that father had sharpened for me the night before. I skinned one side of the animal, but when it came to turning it over, I was too small. I was wondering what to do when I heard my father's voice calling, 'To-ki-i-la-la-hu-wo,' 'Where are you?' I quickly jumped on my pony and rode to the top of a little hill near by. Father saw me and came to me at once. He was so pleased to see me and glad to know that I was safe. I knew that I could never lie to my father. He was too fond of me and I too proud of him. He had always told me to tell the truth. He wanted me to be an honest man, so I resolved then to tell the truth even if it took from me a little glory. He rode up to me with a glad expression on his face, expecting me to go back with him to his kill. As he came up, I said as calmly as I could, 'Father, I have killed a buffalo.' His smile changed to surprise and he asked me where my buffalo was. I pointed to it and we rode over to where it lay, partly skinned.

Father set to work to skin it for me. I had watched him do this many times and knew perfectly well how to do it myself, but I could not turn the animal over. There was a way to turn the head of the animal so that the body would be balanced on the back while being skinned. Father did this for me, while I helped all I could. When the hide was off, father put it on the pony's back with the hair side next to the pony. On this he arranged the meat so it would balance.

Then he covered the meat carefully with the rest of the hide, so no dust would reach it while we traveled home. I rode home on top of the load.

I showed my father the arrows that I had used and just where the animal had been hit. He was very pleased and praised me over and over again. I felt more glad than ever that I had told the truth and I have never regretted it. I am more proud now that I told the truth than I am of killing the buffalo.

We then rode to where my father had killed a buffalo. There we stopped and prepared it for taking home. It was late afternoon when we got back to camp. No king ever rode in state who was more proud than I that day as I came into the village sitting high up on my load of buffalo meat. Mother had now two hunters in the family and I knew how she was going to make over me. It is not customary for Indian men to brag about their exploits and I had been taught that bragging was not nice. So I was very quiet, although I was bursting with pride. Always when arriving home I would run out to play, for I loved to be with the other boys, but this day I lingered about close to the tipi so I could hear the nice things that were said about me. It was soon all over camp that Ota K'te had killed a buffalo.

My father was so proud that he gave away a fine horse. He called an old man to our tipi to cry out the news to the rest of the people in camp. The old man stood at the door of our tipi and sang a song of praise to my father. The horse had been led up and I stood holding it by a rope. The old man who was doing the singing called the other old man who was to receive the horse as a present. He accepted the horse by coming up to me, holding out his hands to me, and saying, 'Ha-ye,' which means 'Thank you.' The old man went away very grateful for the horse.

That ended my first and last buffalo hunt. It lives only in my memory, for the days of the buffalo are over.

THE END

CPSIA information can be obtained
at www.ICGtesting.com
Printed in the USA
LVHW041209200223
739760LV00004B/10

9 780803 293342